ISBN: 1499114117
ISBN 13: 9781499114119
Library of Congress Control Number: XXXXX (If applicable)
LCCN Imprint Name: City and State (If applicable)

Dedication

We dedicate this work to our Shekinah Glory Christian Church family and all the lives that have helped shape our understanding of God's love.

We are grateful for having had the opportunity to shepherd you, leading you to and through life-transforming experiences: salvation, deliverance, recovery and stabilization. It is our prayer that those that we have served, at church, in schools, in the marketplaces around the world, would exercise their full privilege in Christ and choose to live out their lives to the glory of God.

Contents

Preface

God placed this phrase in my spirit: "born again." The believer who has accepted Jesus Christ as his Lord and Savior has experienced a transformation called a "new birth." John 3:3 says, "Jesus answered and said to him, 'Most assuredly, I say to you, unless one is born again, he cannot see the kingdom of God'" (NKJV).[1] This new birth has caused him to be a "new creation." 2 Corinthians 5:17 says, "Therefore, if anyone is in Christ, he a new creation; old things have passed away; behold, all things have become new" (NKJV). Therefore this new creation has become born again. The born again is a person. This is the identity of the community of believers. So, a believer in Jesus Christ who has experienced the new birth has become a born again believer.

There are many people who believe in Jesus who are not born again. The Bible says in James 2:19, "You believe that there is one God; you do well: Even the demons believe, and tremble" (NKJV). It is not enough just to believe in one God or to believe that Jesus is the Son of God. Why? Because the Bible says, "And demons also came out of many, crying out, and saying, 'you are the Christ the Son of God!' And He rebuking them did not allow them to speak: for they knew that he was the Christ" (Luke 4:41 NKJV). So we need to understand that we must be born again.

I will be using 'born again' as a noun. What is a noun? It is the name of a person, place, thing, or idea. Whatever exists, we assume, can be named—and that name is a noun.

There are many people today who say that they are a Christian, however, they do not consider themselves born again. They will make statements like this:

"I believe that Jesus Christ is the Son of God and that he died for my sins."
"Are you born again?" I would reply.
"Born again? What is that?" they would answer. .

Many would reply as though being born again is some kind of occult religion. Someone once asked my wife, "You are not one of those born again people, are you?" Some will even say, "I am a believer in Christ. I have repented for my sins, and I am saved. I do not believe that I will become born again until I die. When I am resurrected, I will be born again, and I will go to heaven."

There are many people who have accepted Jesus as their Savior, but not as their Lord. They want to be saved from eternal hell, but they do not want Jesus to be Lord over their life.

For example, I use this analogy as if life is like a car, and this car is driving down a cliff, heading toward destruction. They are in fear for their life, so they call on the name of Jesus to save them. He comes into the car, takes the steering wheel, and steers the car to safety, and they are saved. Now Jesus is saying, "I want to be Lord of your life; you can stay in the passenger's seat, and I will continue to direct your life," and the reply is, "No, thank you, Jesus. I know you saved me, however, I do not want you to be Lord of my life." Wow, this is what many people say subconsciously: "Jesus, I will take the steering wheel now, and you can get in the backseat. I will drive this vehicle (my life) where I want it to go."

Romans 10:9 says, "If you confess with your mouth the Lord Jesus, and believe in your heart that God has raised him from the dead, you will be saved" (NKJV). Affirming the Lordship of Jesus is central to our salvation. Confessing Jesus as Lord has two basic components. One is our relationship to Jesus. The other is who Jesus really is.

Jesus himself said in John 3:3, "I say unto thee, except a man be born again, he cannot see the kingdom of God."

These ideas regarding the born again have prompted my wife and I to write this book by the leading of the Holy Spirit.

Introduction

"I hate you, and I never want to see you again. I will never forgive you. I don't care anything about you; in fact, you can go to hell!"

Wow! How often I have heard these words from those who say they are born again.

Who is really saying these words? Is it truly the one born again, or is it coming from the old man, the false-identity self? How can a person who is born again hate? How can a born again person live with unforgiveness? How can a born again person tell someone that he or she can go to hell?

You have been told over and over again that you are a Christian and that you should not say or do such things. You tell people that you are only human or "that is just who I am." You say that you are born again—and you are. You go to church and may even be a leader in your church. You try to live a good Christian life, yet you keep doing things you don't want to do. Hmm...sounds like something I have heard before. I even read about it in the Bible.

These are the things that we want to look at in this book. We want to explore and talk about "Living out of your born again self."

CHAPTER ONE

Living Out Of Your Born Again Self

First we must know what it means to be born again. I have personally met many church goers who cannot articulate what this means.

I often ask the Christians I've met, "Are you born again?" This question should bring joy, to the contrary, there are some who become offended by being asked such a question. I have even encountered some Christians who have become offended when I would ask them; "Are you born-again," because they were living contrary to what the Bible has to say. But the life of a Christian is beautiful, and should draw others to ask; "there is something different about you, what is it?"

What a great way to win souls for Christ, by our testimony, sharing our born again experience.

I Am the God That You Have Been Looking For

I vividly remember my born again experience. It was in a small church in Dallas, Texas. My twin sister took me to her church. As I entered, I sat at the back. Everyone was singing, praising, and worshipping God. Suddenly, a man sitting in the last row behind me began to speak in a strange way. As he continued, I could feel something; I sensed that he was somehow talking to me, but I could not understand his words. Then I heard a voice within me say, "I am the God that you have been looking for; I am the God of Abraham, Isaac, and Jacob. I am your God." This experience was surreal to me since at the time I was a practicing Muslim. And Islam taught us to believe in Ishmael as the promised child or child of sacrifice. As a Muslim, I believed that Ishmael was the firstborn and the child that was offered as a sacrifice to God. I sat there wrestling with my thoughts and what I clearly heard repeat itself from within me was, "I am the God of Abraham, Isaac, and Jacob. I am your God."

At that very moment I was moved to accept the authority of Jesus Christ and embrace Him as my Savior. Even today, I do not remember anything the pastor said. I only remember the end of his message, and somehow I found myself at the front of the church. Standing there, the pastor asked me, "Why are you here at the altar? What do you want from God?"

I replied, "I do not understand this concept of the Trinity—God being three in one—I just do not understand." He said to me, "Understanding will come later. You must first accept Jesus Christ by faith."

The pastor led me in the prayer of faith found in the Bible that says, "If you confess with your mouth the Lord Jesus and believe in your heart that God raised Him from the dead, you will be saved" (Romans 10:9 NKJV). Then he led me in a prayer of acceptance of the free gift of salvation given to us through the authority of Jesus Christ. After praying that prayer, I felt a ton of weight being lifted off of me. I knew that I was a changed man inside. I knew I no longer had to try to be good enough to please God to get to heaven. I knew I was born again.

That day, I made a decision to accept Jesus not only as my Savior, but also as my Lord: he became Lord over my life and my Master. I wanted to live the rest my life serving and pleasing Him.

2

I'm Glad I Know Salvation is Free

My wife says her born again experience happened when she was seventeen years old. I quote:

"I was singing with a Gospel singing group that would sing at different kinds of services. After a wonderful service of singing, our group went out to eat. I arrived home late that night. My parents were asleep, and the house was quiet. I went into the bathroom and started to get ready for bed. I began to hum one of the songs that we had ministered that evening. It was entitled, "I'm Glad I Know Salvation is Free." As I started humming and singing, the power of God began to fill the room, and His presence began to fill me. I found myself with my hands up, down on my knees, singing at the top of my lungs, "I'm glad I know salvation is free!" At that moment, I gave my life to Jesus Christ... on the floor in the bathroom late at night, while my parents were asleep.

I was not in the church during service; there was no great big choir, no preacher preaching and saying, 'come take my hand.' It was just me and God in the bathroom. I was lying on the floor. At that moment, I knew Jesus came into my life, and I knew He came into my heart. I knew my life was changed. Suddenly my mother came to the door and said, "What's going on?" I turned around and looked at her with my eyes filled with tears and my voice trembling with fear and with awe. I said, "Mommy, I know I'm saved. Jesus died for me, and now I'm saved."

How about you? Are you born again? Maybe the above experiences are not yours; however, you do have your own unique experience. God changed your life so that you can tell someone about the transforming power of Jesus Christ. Do not keep this good news to yourself, but share it with everyone that God leads you to share it with.

As Christians, We Must First Know What It means to be Born Again

Let's look at what the Bible has to say:

> "There was a man of the Pharisees named Nicodemus, a ruler of the Jews: This man came to Jesus by night, and said to him, "Rabbi, we know that You are a teacher come from God; for no one can do these signs that You do, unless God is with him."
> Jesus answered and said unto him, "Most assuredly, I say to you, unless one is born again, he cannot see the kingdom of God."
> Nicodemus said to him, "How can a man be born when he is old? Can he enter a second time into his mother's womb, and be born?"
> Jesus answered, "Most assuredly I say to you, unless one is born of water and the Spirit, he cannot enter into the kingdom of God. That which is born of the flesh is flesh, and that which is born of the Spirit is spirit. Do not marvel that I said to you, 'You must be born again.' The wind blows where it wishes, and you hear the sound of it, but cannot tell where it comes from and where it goes. So it is with everyone who is born of the Spirit."

Nicodemus answered and said to him, "How can these things be?"

Jesus answered and said to him, "Art you the teacher of Israel, and do not know these things? Most assuredly, I say to you, we speak what we know, and testify what we have seen; and you do not receive our witness. If I have told you earthly things, and you do not believe, how will you believe, if I tell you of heavenly things?" (John 3:1–12 NKJV)

There are five key things that Jesus is telling us.

1. The first key is found in verse 3: Man must be born again.
   There must be a rebirth. (We will explain that later.)

2. The second key is found in verse 5: Born of water.
   Water represents the word; Jesus is the word in the flesh. (We will talk more about that later.)

3. The third key is also found in verse 5: Born of the Holy Spirit.
   You must receive a new spirit.

4. The fourth key is found in verse 6: Born of flesh. We will talk more about that later.

5. The fifth key is found in verse 7: Marvel not.

In order for us to understand what Jesus was saying to Nicodemus and is saying to us today, we must go back and look at what the Bible says in Genesis: "And God said, 'Let us make man in our image, after our likeness'" (Genesis 1:26). Man was created an eternal being, perfect and with no sin. It was not until the fall of man that man needed to be born again. Genesis 3: 1–24 tells the whole story of the fall of man.

Man, Like God, is a Triune Being

"God is a Spirit" (John 4:24). God made us in his image; since God is a Spirit, we are also a spirit being.

Man, like God, is a triune being. Apostle Paul stated in 1 Thessalonians 5:23, "The very God of peace sanctify you wholly and I pray God your whole spirit and soul and body be preserved blameless unto the coming of our Lord Jesus Christ." This verse clearly divides a person into three parts, as follows:

1. Spirit
2. Soul
3. Body

"And the Lord God formed man of the dust of the ground and breathed into his nostrils the breath of life; and man became a living soul" (Genesis 2:7). The word "breathed" in Hebrew is *naphach* (naw-fakh'). This is a primitive root word meaning "to puff," in various applications, literally "to inflate," or "to blow hard." The verse goes on to say 'into his nostrils, God breathed the breath of life;' "breath" in the Hebrew is *neshamah* (nesh-aw-maw'), meaning "divine inspiration," "intellect," "soul," or "spirit." The verse says 'man became a living soul.' "Soul" in the Hebrew is *neshamah* (nesh-aw-maw'), meaning "a breathing creature" or "a thinking being."[2]

In the beginning, God created the figure of a man with the dust of the earth and breathed into his nostrils "the breath of life." When the breath of life came in contact with man's body, the soul was made. The soul, which is made up of the mind, emotions, appetite, desires, and passions, are the consummation of man's body and his spirit. This spirit (*pneuma*) is the vital principal by which the body is animated. It is the rational part of man, and the power by which a human being thinks, feels, and decides. This is why the Bible calls man a living soul. This breath of life is man's spirit, the source of man's life. This breath of life comes from the Creator. However, we should not confuse this spirit called breath of life with the Holy Spirit of God. There is a difference between the Holy Spirit and the human spirit. The human spirit is in the innermost core of the human soul. When we are conceived and then born physically, our spirit functions on a natural plain.

The word "life" in Genesis 2:7, "the breath of life," is *chay* (khah'-ee), meaning, 'alive.' It is a plurality of life. This tells us that God's breathing produces the following two kinds of life:

1. Spiritual
2. Soul-ish

So now we see when God's breath of life entered the man of clay, he became a spirit. God describes the two types of life as follows:

Spiritual Life
The spiritual nature of humans processes higher faculties and differs from that of animals, especially in the areas of intellect and free will. God, who has thoughts far above our human capacity for thought, chose to share his divine essence with humans through the gifts of intellect and free will. In this way, all human beings have been given the aptitude for knowing and loving God.

This is the source of dignity, meaning that each human being is created in the image of God as an expression of his great love for us. God breathed into human nature His own image and likeness. Whether male or female, young or old, productive or unproductive, believer or unbeliever, every person is created in the image of God.

At the same time, when this spirit came into contact with the body, it produced the human soul.

Soul-ish Life/The Human Soul
This is the life principle that animates the human body.

It is unique to each person, meaning that it is the personality and the individuality of each person.

It is immaterial, meaning that it cannot be perceived objectively by the senses. Subjectively we can "see" the effect of the presence of the soul in a live body and the absence of the soul in a cadaver.

It is immortal, meaning that it continues to exist even after the body dies. Therefore the soul does not depend upon the body for its being or its activity. However, while the soul and body are joined, the soul maintains some dependence upon the body, for it needs the body's senses to provide it with information to which to respond.

Your soul consists with the following three main faculties:

1. Free will: the ability to choose, to decide
2. Intellect: the ability to think, to reason, to imagine, to remember
3. Emotion: the ability to desire, to experience feelings

As mentioned before, man is a spirit-being. He possesses a physical body in which he dwells. He has a soul composed of his reasoning faculties. His body enables him to contact physical things. His reasoning faculties contact mental things. And his spirit contacts spiritual things.

Now this spirit that man received in the beginning is not the life of God that we receive at the time of our regeneration (what I call being born again). The life that we receive at the time of regeneration is the life of God Himself, the Born Again Life. It is the life represented by the tree of life mentioned in Genesis 3:24. The spirit of man (human spirit) is eternal, but it does not have eternal life.

Meaning that before man receives eternal life; his spirit is dominated by spiritual death.

What Is Spiritual Death?
It is broken fellowship with God. In Genesis 2:17, God tells Adam that in the day he eats of the forbidden fruit, he will "surely die." Adam does die, but his physical death does not occur immediately: God had another type of death in mind— spiritual death. This separation is a broken fellowship with God. It is exactly what we see in Genesis 3:8. When Adam and Eve heard the voice of the Lord, they hid themselves from the presence of God. The fellowship had been broken. They were spiritually dead. 1 Corinthians 2:14 says, "But the natural man does not receive the things of the Spirit of God for they are foolishness unto him; nor can they know them because they are spiritually discerned" (NKJV).

Because man sinned, we have been separated from God. However, God could not deny Himself. He looked into the earth and saw an image of Himself that he has placed in mankind. Therefore, God searched for the image He first placed in humanity and motivated by His love towards mankind, was compelled to rescue His likeness through the person of His only begotten Son, who is the divine bridge of eternal life between us and God. Jesus, our Hope of Salvation, demolished spiritual death once He yielded to the cross for us.

Rabbi, We Know that You are a Teacher Come from God

Now let us go back to the story in John 3:1–12 when Jesus and Nicodemus were conversing. Before we go to this conversation, you need to know who Nicodemus was.

[3]Nicodemus was a noble Jewish leader and a scholar of the Jewish law. Jesus not only attracted ordinary men but scholars as well. The beliefs of the Pharisees, and the peculiarities of their sect, were directly contrary to the spirit of Christianity. He was a ruler of the Jews, a member of the great Sanhedrin, a statesman, a counselor, and a man of authority in Jerusalem. However, when he came to Jesus by night, he did not come to talk about politics and state affairs. No, he came to talk about the concerns of his own soul and its salvation, and, without a roundabout way, comes immediately to the main point. He calls Christ "rabbi," which signifies a great man. This is appropriate given that Isaiah 19:20 states, "And He shall send them a Savior and mighty one, and He will deliver them" (NKJV).

The Jews believed the words of the prophet Isaiah, and were looking for a Savior, whom they believed would be the Messiah.

Now listen to the response that Nicodemus gives:

His ability to perceive: "He said unto him, Rabbi (teacher), we know that you are a teacher come from God" In John 3:2 (NKJV). He calls Christ a teacher who comes from God; not educated nor ordained by men as other teachers, but supported with divine inspiration and divine authority. Christ came to be the sovereign ruler, he came first to be a teacher by the power of truth, not by the sword.

His confidence of it: He says in effect, 'we know; and not only I, but others: we cannot deny this truth it was plain and self-evident.' He may have known that there were others of the Pharisees and rulers with whom he conversed that were under the same convictions but had not the courage to come forth. There were others who were under the same conviction because he spoke in the plural number. "We know," yet he came to receive instructions from Christ. "Master teacher," he said, "we come with a desire to be taught, to be your scholars, for we are fully satisfied you are a divine teacher" (paraphrased).

The ground of his confidence: John 3:2 says, "For no man can do these signs that you do, unless God be with him" (NKJV). He was declaring that they were confident of the truth of Christ's miracles and that they were not counterfeit.

Here was Nicodemus—a man of great prudence, an inquisitive man, one that had all the reason and opportunity imaginable to examine these events—so fully satisfied that they were real miracles that he was amazed by them to go contrary to his own interest, and contrary to the stream of those of his own rank, who were prejudiced against Christ. Therefore, not only Nicodemus, but we, too, should receive him as a teacher come from God. His miracles were and still are Jesus' credentials. The course of nature could not be altered but by the power of the God of nature, whom we are sure is the God of truth and goodness - and would never set his seal to a lie or a cheat.

The master teacher gives a direct and significant answer to Nicodemus's address. Jesus answered in John 3:3, "Most assuredly I say to you, unless one is born again he cannot see the kingdom of God" (NKJV).

His answer was a rebuke of what he saw as defective in the address of Nicodemus: It was not enough for him to admire Christ's miracles.

It is plain that Nicodemus expected the kingdom of heaven and the Messiah to come. It was a common notion of the Jews. He had expected it to appear in external pomp and power. He doubts not that this Jesus, who works miracles, is either the Messiah or a prophet. Nicodemus, like others today, wants to compliment Jesus on what he can do so that they can share in the kingdom.

However, Christ tells Nicodemus that he can share none of the benefits unless there is a change of the spirit, of the principles and dispositions, equivalent to a new birth.

What is Jesus saying to Nicodemus and to us as Christians today? That we must be born again.

What is required to be born again?
There must be a rebirth; we must receive and live a new life. Birth is the beginning of life; to be born again is to begin anew. We cannot patch up the old self. We must have a new nature, new principles, new affections, and new aims.

If You Had the Chance to Live Your Life All Over Again, Would You Choose to Be…

One day, I was talking to a Christian brother, and he said, "I am gay, and I was born this way, and God accepts me as I am because he is the one who made me."

I replied, "Do you believe that you were born in sin?"

"Yes," he said.

"OK," I said, "then you must believe when Jesus said you must be born again to see the kingdom of heaven. My question to you is, 'Are you born again?"

"Yes."

I said to him, "Good. Then I have another question for you. If you had the chance to live your life all over again, would you choose to be gay?" "Of course not; I am gay because I was born this way."

"Well, God loves you so much that he has given you another chance to start your life all over again. That is what Jesus meant when he said you must be born again. He has given you a new birth and a new nature. He has given you new principles, new affections, and new aims."

By our first birth, we are corrupt, shaped in sin and iniquity. The Bible makes this very clear with the story of King David's fall. King David who is described in the scriptures as 'a man after God's own heart', committed adultery and impregnated another man's wife. Therefore, in an attempt to cover his sin, he had the man killed. David cries out to God to have mercy on him. He essentially tells God, 'I was born in sin and I desire the truth; purge me and wash me whiter than snow.' David wrote in Psalms 51:5-10, "Behold, I was shapen in iniquity; and in sin did my mother conceive me. Behold, thou desirest truth in the inward parts: and in the hidden part thou shalt make me to know wisdom. Purge me with hyssop, and I shall be clean: wash me, and I shall be whiter than snow. Make me to hear joy and gladness; that the bones which thou hast broken may rejoice. Hide thy face from my sins, and blot out all mine iniquities. Create in me a clean heart, O God; and renew a right spirit within me." (KJV)

Now let's go back to the story of Nicodemus. Jesus talks about the indispensable necessity of the new birth when he says "except a man is born again." Any person that partakes of the human nature will consequently partake of its corruptions. Therefore, they cannot see the kingdom of God unless they are born again. Regeneration is absolutely necessary to please and to see God.

Listen to Nicodemus's opposition toward Christ's statement. "How can a man be born when he is old? Can he enter the second time into his mother's womb, and be born?" (John 3:4)

He is now showing his weakness of knowledge; what Christ spoke of spiritually he seems to have understood in a corporal and carnal manner, as if there was no other way of regenerating an immoral soul than by reframing the body. He is speaking as if there was such a connection between the soul and the body that there could be no fashioning of the heart anew but by forming the bones anew. Nicodemus, as others do today, valued the first birth with its dignities and rights.[3]

Apostle Paul could have gloried in the flesh, but look at what he says in Philippians 3:3–9:

> "For we are the circumcision, who worship by the Spirit of God and glory in Christ Jesus and put no confidence in the flesh. Though I myself have

reason for confidence in the flesh also. If anyone else thinks he has reason for confidence in the flesh, I have more: circumcised on the eighth day, of the people of Israel, of the tribe of Benjamin, as to the law, a Pharisee; as to zeal, a persecutor of the church; as to righteousness under the law, blameless. But whatever gain I had, I count everything as loss because of the surpassing worth of knowing Christ Jesus my Lord. For His sake I have suffered the loss of all things and count them as rubbish, in order that I may gain Christ and be found in Him, not having a righteousness of my own that comes from the law, but that which comes through faith in Christ, the righteousness from God that depends on faith" (ESV).[4]

Nicodemus was astonished to hear that he must be born again. After all, he was of great breeding—born an Israelite, there was no other birth that stood a fairer place in that time and culture. However, we see that Paul made it very clear that he has no confidence in his own flesh as being righteous before God. Indeed, they looked poorly upon a Gentile, or in our day and time, an unlearned, uncultured, or a nonreligious person. But there is a need to be born again. It is as if Nicodemus was saying, "How can I—a Pharisee, a Jew, a good person—be any better?" There are many people today who feel the same way.

Nicodemus' willingness to be taught: He does not turn his back on Christ because of his hard saying, but ingenuously acknowledges his ignorance, which implies a desire to be better informed.

Nicodemus gives up and asks, "Lord, make me to understand, for this is very puzzling."[5] He goes on to say in John verse 4,

"How can a man be born when he is old? Can he enter the second time into his mother's womb, and be born?" Many of us today need to ask the same question: "Lord, I want to know how I can be born again. I want to know—how can I have a new life?"

Jesus answered Nicodemus, as he is telling us the same thing today. John 3:5 says, "Except a man be born of water and of the Spirit, he cannot enter into the kingdom of God."

Jesus knew that John the Baptist came baptizing in water, saying, "Repent ye: for the kingdom of heaven is at hand" (Matthew 3:2). John goes on to say in Matthew 3:11, "I indeed baptize you with water unto repentance: but he that cometh after me is mightier than I...he shall baptize you with the Holy Ghost [Spirit] and with fire.

Physical Water Cannot Wash Away Our Sins

The regenerating work of the Spirit is referred to as water: "Except a man be born of water..." (John 3:5). To be born again is to be born of water (washing of the Word of God), and of the Spirit, that is, of the Spirit working like water, as in Matthew 3:11: "with the Holy Ghost and fire." With fire means with the Holy Spirit as with fire. The Spirit sanctifies the soul; He cleanses and purifies it as water, takes away its filth, because it was unfit for the kingdom of God. It is "the washing of regeneration," according to Titus 3:5, "not by works of righteousness, which we have done, but according to his mercy he saved us, by the washing of regeneration, and renewing of the Holy Ghost."[6]

The nature of this change is by the Spirit. Those who are regenerated are made spiritual and refined like the taking

16

away of waste products off of molten metal during smelting process. I have seen this many times on my own job, by the heating up of a smelting pot. We would take pure lead and heat it at a high temperature in a huge pot, and then all of the impurities would rise up to the top. We would then take a large spoon and scoop up all of the waste products, or impurities, and throw them away. Likewise, there must be a separating of the dregs of sinful desire so that dictates and interests of the rational and immortal soul achieve the dominion it should have over the flesh.

This change is a must. Christ shows that it is necessary for the nature of man for we are not fit to enter into the kingdom of God until we are born again. He states in John 3:6, "That which is born of the flesh is flesh." Here is the disorder of the sinful flesh. Because of this deadly sickness, it is plain to see there is no cure except that we must be born again.

The soul is still spiritual substance, so wedded to the flesh, so captivated by the will of the flesh, so in love with the delights of the flesh, so employed in making provision for the flesh, that it is mostly called flesh; it is carnal. How can there be communion between God, who is a Spirit, and a soul in this condition? The first man, Adam fell in sin; therefore, all after him are born in sin. The Bible says "For as in Adam, all die" (1 Corinthians 15:22). Therefore, this corrupt nature, which is the flesh, takes rise from our first birth. The new nature (I call this our born again self), which is spirit, must rise from a second birth. First Corinthians 15:22 says, "Even so, in Christ, all shall be made alive."[7]

There Must Be Another Original

Nicodemus spoke of entering again into his mother's womb and being born again. So this is with you and me today. If we were to have the chance to be born again in the flesh, what purpose would it serve? I have said many times that I wish I could live my life all over again. If Nicodemus or any of us were born again in the flesh a hundred times, that would not mend the matter, for still that which is born of flesh is flesh; a clean thing cannot be brought out of an unclean thing. There must be another original, born of the Spirit, or we cannot become spiritually connected to God.[8]

My point is that God made man consisting of body and soul, yet in the beginning, his spiritual part had so much dominion over his corporeal part, he was pronounced a living soul: "And man became a living soul" (Genesis 2:7). Adam was not called man in the beginning; he was called a living soul. This living soul began by indulging the appetites of the flesh. He prostituted the just dominion of the soul to the tyranny of sensual lust and became no longer a living soul, but flesh: "For dust thou art" (Genesis 3:19). Adam became a dust man, a man of the flesh. The living soul became dead and inactive, as it says in the Bible, "And the LORD God commanded the man, saying; of every tree of the garden thou mayest freely eat: But of the tree of the knowledge of good and evil, thou shalt not eat of it: for in the day that thou eatest thereof thou shalt surely die" (Genesis 2:16–17). (KJV)

And so Adam, and consequentially all of mankind, became earthly, fleshly, and carnal. In this degenerate state, he begat a son in his own likeness; he transmitted the human nature, which had been entirely deposited in his hands, thus corrupted and depraved. It is still being propagated. We are all born in sin. There is nothing we can do about it. It is not enough to put on new clothes; we must be born again.

Marvel Not

"Marvel not that I said unto thee, ye must be born again" (John 3:7).

What does the word "marvel" mean? According to the Merriam Webster dictionary, it means "to wonder" or "to marvel" It is to feel amazement or bafflement about something. We should not marvel at it, for when we consider the holiness of God and the great design of our redemption, the depravity of our nature, and the constitution of the happiness set before us, we should not think it strange that so must stress is laid upon this as the one thing needful: that we must be born again.

It seems to Nicodemus that the words of Jesus are very peculiar. "Do not marvel that I said to you, you must be born again. The wind blows where it wishes, and you hear its sound, but you do not know where it goes. So it is with everyone who is born of the Spirit.' Nicodemus said to him, 'How can these things be?'" (John 3:7–9 ESV)

Many are still asking the same question today: "How can this be?"

How Can These Things Be?

Nicodemus admits his ignorance to the meaning of the teaching of Jesus. How can these things be? How many of us will admit our ignorance of what the Bible is telling us? The things of the Spirit of God are foolishness to the natural man.

The natural man is estranged from them, and they are dark to him, and he is prejudiced against them; therefore, they are foolishness to him. Because this doctrine sounded unintelligible, Nicodemus questions the truth of it because it seemed like a paradox. Many of us today have such a high opinion of our own capacity to think that whatever cannot be proven cannot be believed.

Listen to the reproof that Christ gave him for his dullness and ignorance: "Art thou a master of Israel, and knowest not these things?" (John 3:10 KJV) Wow! A "master," which is *didaskalos* in the Greek, is a "doctor," "master teacher," or "a tutor." Here is one who sits in Moses' chair, yet is not only unacquainted with the doctrine of regeneration, but also incapable of understanding it. This word is a reproof to those who undertake teaching others, yet are ignorant and unskillful in the word.[9]

The truth that Christ taught was very certain: "Truly, truly, I say to you, we speak of what we know, and bear witness to what we have seen, but you do not receive our testimony. If I have told you earthly things and you do not believe, how can you believe if I tell you heavenly things?" (John 3:12 ESV)

And You Hear Its Sound

"The wind bloweth where it listeth, and thou hearest the sound thereof, but canst not tell whence it cometh, and whither it goeth: so is every one that is born of the Spirit" (John 3:8 KJV).

Jesus uses the wind as a metaphor for the Spirit. The wind blows where it wishes. The same word in the Greek (*pneuma*) signifies both the wind and the Spirit. This comparison is used to show that the Spirit, in regeneration, works arbitrarily, as a free agent. We cannot change the order of the wind nor is it under our command. God directs it; the Spirit fulfills His word. "Fire and hail, snow and clouds, and stormy wind all fulfilling his word" (Psalm 148:8 NKJV). The Spirit dispenses His influences where, when, on whom, and in what measure and degree He pleases, dividing to every man as he wills. The Spirit works powerfully and with evident effects: And you hear its sound, but you do not know where it comes from or where it goes; its causes are hidden, its effects are manifest.

Nicodemus is mystified: How can these things be? Christ, the master teacher and expounder of the necessity of regeneration, made it clearer to him. The corruption of nature that makes it necessary, and the way of the Spirit that makes it practicable, are as much mysteries to Nicodemus as the thing itself; though he had acknowledged Christ as a divine teacher, he still had problems receiving his teachings when they did not agree with the notions he was accustomed to. Even today, many profess the doctrine of Christ in general but will not embrace the truth of the necessity of being born again.

Because this doctrine sounded unintelligible, Nicodemus questioned the truth of it because it seemed like a paradox. Many of us today have such a high opinion of our own capacity to think that whatever cannot be proven cannot be believed.

The Truths of the Gospel are Heavenly Things

The truths Christ taught were communicated in language and expressions borrowed from common and earthly things, yet in their own nature were lofty in thought and heavenly. It is God's desire to communicate with man. God takes from earthly things and, in using similarities, makes these concepts more easy and intelligible, as that of comparing the new birth and the wind. The things of the Gospel are heavenly things—out of the scope of the inquiry by human reason.[10]

None but Christ—not Muhammad, Buddha, or any of the prophets—were able to reveal to us the will of God for our salvation. Nicodemus addressed Christ as a prophet, just like Jews and Muslims today; but he must know, and we all must know, that Christ is greater than all the prophets. He is the *Christos*—the Anointed One, the Messiah, the Son of God. He says "we must be born again."

CHAPTER TWO

The Old Nature Has Been Put To Death

To be born again simply means that the old nature (sinful nature) has been put to death. The sinful nature denotes our personal preferences, likes and dislikes, as well as motives and reasoning that are concerned only with the self and selfish ideas and ways. When we are born again, God gives us a new spirit (nature), causing us to have a new set of ideas and thoughts that govern our lives so that we may make the will of God manifest. We must be saved (the act of receiving salvation) to go to heaven, but to participate in the realm of God in the earth, we must come into the reality of our born again experiences—preferring the ways of God and intentionally demonstrating his ways.

"But the natural man receives not the things of the Spirit of God: for they are foolishness unto him: neither can he know them, because they are spiritually discerned" (1 Corinthians 2:14).

The part of man that is born again (recreated) is his spirit. This recreated spirit (born of God) now directs the soul (heart, mind, will, desires, and preferences).

Ezekiel 11:19–20 is a remarkable prophecy: "And I will give them one heart, and I will put a new spirit within you; and I will take the stony heart out of their flesh, and will give them a heart of flesh."

Our old nature (old heart / soul) was selfish and only wanted to please itself, it did not know how to please God, even the good that we did was to please ourselves, because it made us feel good. The heart is the core of our being that governs all other parts - the mind, emotions, body and soul. It organizes our life through reason, understanding and conscience. It navigates our way. What comes from it reflects its nature. Our old nature cannot please God; it is impossible, because it does not know God. Our old heart does not have the nature or character of God. When I talk about your old heart I am talking about your soul. I am not talking about your heart as an organ.

Therefore, our old nature had to be put to death. We were born in sin and with a deceitful heart in a body of flesh. When we are born again we receive from God a new heart (new nature) a new spirit and his very own life. This new nature directs our heart and we now have the desire to please God.

The Hand of the Lord Reached Into My Body and Pulled Out My Old Heart

Many years ago when I was first born again, I read the previous scripture. I prayed, "Lord, I know that you have given me a new spirit and that I am born again, but you said, 'and I will take the stony heart out of their flesh and will give them (me) a heart of flesh.'" I prayed, "Lord, what is this heart of flesh that you have given me?" That night, I fell into a deep sleep, and I had a vivid dream:

The hand of the Lord reached into my body and pulled out my old heart, and He said, "Look at it." When I looked, it was disgusting, deep black, ugly, and full of sin and disease. I could not bear to look at it. Then immediately, he held in his hand a heart that was white as snow—it was pure, and the look of it made me feel no condemnation. The Lord then gently placed into my body this new heart of flesh.

Hallelujah! Praise God!

God has given the born again a new heart—a heart entirely for the true God and not divided, as it had been, among many gods (things that are contrary to God). This new heart is firmly fixed and resolved for God and not wavering; steady and uniform, and not inconsistent with itself. One heart is a sincere and upright heart, and its intentions are in agreement with its profession. God puts a new spirit within you and gives a new life that is willingly in agreement with the new circumstances into which God, in his providence, would bring. The born again is sanctified (made holy, set apart, rendered legitimate) having a new spirit, quite different from what it was; the born again acts from new principles, walks by new rules, and aims at a new end. A new name or a new face will not serve without a new spirit. "And I will take the stony heart out of their flesh,"

says Ezekiel (Ezekiel 11:19). That night in the dream, the Lord showed me that my old heart of stone was my old, corrupt nature.

The born again heart shall no longer be, as it has been, contaminated and condemned, dead, dry, hard and heavy, or like stony ground. "And I will give them a heart of flesh"...not dead to the things of God and prideful flesh that is always trying to satisfy its fleshly desires, but a flesh that is alive to the reality of Galatians 2:20:

> "I am [my flesh] crucified with Christ: nevertheless I live; [this is a paradox, a statement that seems self-contradictory or absurd but in reality expresses a truth] yet not I, but Christ lives in me: and the life which I now live in the flesh [my born again self] I live by the faith of the Son of God, who loved me, and gave himself for me" (NKJV, emphasis added).

God has made the born-again heart sensitive to spiritual pains and spiritual pleasures, tender and apt to receive Godly impressions. Like a stone, our old heart had no life in it. So the old, unclean heart was removed from its place of ruling our lives, and we are given a new heart that is filled with the life of Christ.

It Is the Zoë Kind of Life

2 Corinthians 5:17 says, "Therefore, if anyone is in Christ, he is a new creation; old things have passed away; behold, all things have become new" (NKJV). What is this new creation? It is our new spirit, our new heart, and our new nature; it is the "Zoë kind of life." What is the Zoë kind of life? It is the Greek word used to express the form of "life" that Jesus gives to His

followers. Jesus states in John 10:10 "I have come that they may have life and that they may have it more abundantly" (NKJV). Spiros Zodhiates in his Greek Word Study defines *zoë* as follows:

> "Life; referring to the principle of life in the spirit and soul. Distinguished from bios, physical life...of which *zoë* is the nobler word, expressing all of the highest and best which Christ is and which He gives to His followers. This is the highest blessing of all creatures. It is the God kind of life. It is the life of God living in our born again self. This *zoë* life has caused us to part take of the tree of life called eternal life or everlasting life with God—it is the life of God."[11]

What is the Life of God?
John 3:36 says, "He that believeth on the Son hath everlasting life (*zoë*); and he that believeth not the Son shall not see life." This scripture tells us that unless man has the life of God, he does not have life. This shows us that only God's life is true life; beside this, no other life can be counted as truly living because only the life of God is divine and eternal.

What Does "Divine" Mean?
Being divine means of God, having the nature of God, or being transcendent and distinctive from all others. Only God is God; only God has the nature of God, and only God is transcendent and distinctive. Therefore, only God is divine. The life of God is God Himself. Since it is God Himself, it naturally has the nature of God.

What Does "Eternal" Mean?
Eternal means uncreated, without beginning or end, existing by itself, and existing unchangeably. Only God is uncreated; only

He is "from eternity;" that is, without beginning or end. Since only God Himself is such, so too is the life that is of God. It is uncreated, without beginning or end, self-existing, ever-existing, and never changing; therefore, the life of God is eternal.

What Is Eternal Life?

"For God so loved the world, that he gave his only begotten Son, that whosoever believeth in him should not perish, but have everlasting life" (John 3:16).

Eternal life is only found in Christ Jesus. Because he is from eternity, He has no beginning or end. Every true Christian that believes in the Son of God consents to Him and confides in Him as well as understands the benefit of being born again has eternal life. This is what Christ came to purchase for us and confer upon us. The born again has received everlasting life, not only in the hereafter, but also now; the deed has been sealed and delivered by Jesus. The born again has the Son of God, and in Him, he or she has life and the Spirit of God, or the essence of this life.

John 3:36 says, "He who believes in the Son has everlasting life; and he who does not believe the Son shall not see life, but the wrath of God abides on him" (NKJV). The nonbeliever shall experience eternal death, that is, eternal separation from God. Because man was created in God's image, that is spirit. The spirit of man is eternal. Because of the sin of mankind he was separated from God. The Bible says in Genesis 3:22 "And the LORD God said, Behold, the man is become as one of us, to know good and evil: and now, lest he put forth his hand, and take also of the tree of life, and eat, and live forever: Therefore the LORD God sent him forth from the garden of Eden..."

It has always been God's plan that man be reconciled back to Him. Therefore, God made that way through His Son Jesus Christ. The Bible says "For God so loved the world that he gave his only begotten Son, that whosoever believeth in him should not perish, but have everlasting life. For God sent not his Son into the world to condemn the world; but that the world through him might be saved" (John 3:16-17).

By rejecting the Son of God, one is rejecting God the Father. Thus the consequences of not believing on the finished work of the Son of God will result in eternal separation from God.

What Is Eternal Death?

Eternal death is the fate that awaits all people who ultimately reject God by rejecting the Gospel of is Son, Jesus Christ, which is the virgin birth, the death on the cross, and the resurrection. By rejecting the Gospel message, they remain in their sin and disobedience. Physical death is a one-time experience. Eternal death, on the other hand, is everlasting. It is a death that continues through eternity, a spiritual death that is experienced on a continual basis. Just as spiritual life, by grace through faith in Christ, is everlasting life, eternal death never ends.

The New Creation is Your New Identity

The new creation is your true self. Your new identity is your born again self, now and forever. This is the part of you loves the Lord and wants to do His will. In your born again self, there is nothing but the love of God. First John 4:8 says, "He who does not love does not know God, for God is love" (NKJV). In your born again self, there is no hate, envy, jealousy, or malice—nothing but the love of God.

Romans 7:2 says, "For I [my born again self-] delight in the law of God according to the inward man" [my new heart] (NKJV, emphasis added). Now God has given us the power to live out our new identity.

By reading this book, you should now know what is your new identity or new self. Ephesians 4:24 says, "And to put on the new self, created to be like God in true righteousness and holiness" (NIV).[12] Please say this out loud: "I am the born again." This is your new self.

The Word of God says that we are a new creation, so in our born again self, we are holy, righteous, and blameless. The real you, the one that will live for eternity, loves God, wants to do His will, and doesn't want to sin.

Our Primary Assignment is to be Reconcilers

So why must we live out of the born again self? Because the nature of being born again enables us to establish the Will of God in our lives. And our primary assignment is to be reconcilers as we have been reconciled to God. Every action is to have a healing, joining, unifying goal, reconnecting man with God or man with man. Every thought, word, and deed that comes from us should be able to stand the "reconciler's test:" Did that bring anybody closer to God or closer to man?

2 Corinthians 5: 18–21 says,

> "And all things are of God, who hath reconciled us to himself by Jesus Christ, and hath given to us the ministry of reconciliation; To wit, that God was in Christ, reconciling the world unto himself, not imputing their trespasses unto them; and hath

committed unto us the word of reconciliation. Now then we are ambassadors for Christ, as though God did beseech you by us: we pray you in Christ's stead, be ye reconciled to God. For he hath made him to be sin for us, who knew no sin; that we might be made the righteousness of God in him."

Reconcilers (the born again) can be trusted to do the will of God, regardless of the circumstances, because they know their assignment. They place greater value on the outcome than the inconvenience that may be necessary to bring about the outcome. When you live out of your born again self, you will have to first acknowledge that your way is not God's way, and then choose God's way no matter how challenging, or unpopular, or unlike you it is. You have to say no to yourself (your false-identity self) and deliberately embrace the ways of God because you want to please Him and fulfill your assignment.

Stop Saying "I Am a Sinner Saved by Grace"

So how do we live out of the born again self? You must first know that you are not a sinner saved by grace. Your identity is no longer "sinner" because you have been made (by the virtue of Christ's death on the cross and the resurrection power of God) the righteousness of God, according to 1 Corinthians 5:21. Therefore you are the born again, a new creation. Praise God! You are saved by grace and have been given a new heart and a new spirit. You are, right now, the righteousness of God; you have been placed in right standing with him.

Stop saying, "I am a sinner saved by grace" because the statement, "I am a sinner" has power; with this phrase, you are saying who it is that you are, whether you add "saved by grace" or not. If you believe it, it will keep you from living out of your born again self. Remember 1 Corinthians 5:17, "Therefore, if anyone is in Christ he is a new creation; old things have passed away; behold all things have become new" (NKJV). Whatever you believe about yourself you will live out. If you do not know your true identity, you will be living out of your false-identity self and it will cause you to miss out on fulfilling the purposes and destiny that God has for your life.

Romans 7:24-25 says, "O wretched man that I am! Who shall deliver me from the body of this death? I thank God through Jesus Christ our Lord. So then with the mind I myself serve the law of God; but with the flesh the law of sin."

You must come into the realization that your false-identity self (the old nature) is dead, and Jesus Christ has delivered you from your old self. You must have a change of mind:

> "And be renewed [having a born again experience] in the spirit of your mind; And that ye put on the new man, [the born again] which after God is created in righteousness and true holiness" (Ephesians 4:24, emphasis added).

Your Flesh is Not the Real You

I will never forget an experience I had many years ago. I heard this old preacher say, "Satan has many sons and daughters in the earth. Every time you look in the mirror, you are looking at the son or daughter of Satan." Wow! Your flesh is not the real you; it is your false-identity self. Paul said in Romans 7:25, "...So then with the mind I myself serve the law of God; but with the flesh the law of sin." In other words, you must make a decision to change the way you think. Your mind belongs to God. You have to make a decision that you will not allow your mind to serve Satan. Your flesh, unchecked, will always yield to sin. It's under the gravitational pull of satisfying its fleshly desires because the mind of the flesh is enmity (an enemy) against God. The Bible says in Romans 8:7, "Because the carnal mind is enmity against God: for it is not subject to the law of God, neither indeed can be. So then they that are in the flesh cannot please God."

We must live out of our born again self, not out of our flesh. Why? Because we have been delivered from the body of this death (the law of sin and death). We are no longer a wretched man. We must stand on the word given in Romans 8: 1–3:

"There is therefore now no condemnation to them, which are in Christ Jesus, who walk not after the flesh but after the spirit: For the law of the Spirit of life in Christ Jesus has made me free from the law of sin and death. For what the law could not do, in that it was weak through the flesh, God sending his own son in the likeness of sinful flesh, and for sin, condemned sin in the flesh."

Not Guilty. Let Him Go Free!

Apostle Paul makes it very clear that we are no longer condemned. I say, "Not guilty. Let him go free!" Now what would those words mean if you were on death row? The fact is the whole human race is on death row, justly condemned for repeatedly breaking God's holy law. Without Jesus, we would have no hope at all, but thank God that He has declared us not guilty because he took all of our sins—past, present, and future—and placed them on His body and it was nailed to the cross. Therefore He has offered us freedom from the power of sin and death. Paul does not say, "There is nothing in us that deserves condemnation," (that is in our false-identity self) for there is, and we see it, but it shall not bring us to ruin. There is a cross, afflictions, and displeasures we must bear, but no condemnation. The Lord will chasten us, but we are not condemned with the world. We are under no condemnation by virtue of our union with Christ.

This is the triumph after the complaints and conflict that Paul had, and you and I have, when we go through the vexing, disturbing trials of the sin of self-righteousness. It is an unspeakable privilege and comfort to all of us that are in Christ Jesus that there is "therefore now no condemnation to them which are in Christ Jesus, who walk not after the flesh but after the spirit" (Romans 8:1). I want to make it clear that Paul does not say, "There is no accusation against them," for there is accusation against all, but praise God that the accusation is thrown out, and the indictment squashed.

After eighteen years of prison ministry and preaching this Gospel, I have seen many inmates come to the saving knowledge of Jesus Christ. Many of them were condemned criminals in the natural and spiritual. But praise God! They accepted Jesus Christ as their Savior and were born again.

This Young Man Fell to His Knees and Began to Weep

Many years ago, I received a call from a woman whose son was recently incarcerated for killing another person. She said to me, "Reverend Johnson, please go to the jail and see my son— he was beaten and placed in the medical unit of the jail and is on 24-hour suicide watch." That day, I went to visit the young man and was taken to the area where he was being held. I was allowed to see him and talk to him. His eyes were blackened and partially closed, and his lips were swollen. He stared at me in deep despair. I began to share with him that Jesus died on the cross for his past, present, and future sins and that there was nothing that he could do that God would not forgive him for if he would just repent for what he had done and ask God to forgive him. This young man fell to his knees, began to weep, and said, "You mean to tell me that God will forgive me for this murder, and I do not have to go to hell?" I replied, "Yes, God will forgive you, and you will not end up in hell." That day, the young man received Jesus as his Savior and received no condemnation from God.

Praise God! Hallelujah!

God did not send His Son into the world to condemn it. All sin is condemned by God. God loves the world, in spite of its profound sin. God loves mankind, and doesn't want any to perish, but all to come to the saving knowledge of the Son. To "believe on the name of the Son of God," is nothing less than to believe in Jesus, who He is, and what He did for us, to accept Him, and enter fully into the new birth He offers.

That day this young man became born again and was given a new nature: in spite of being in prison and living a life of hardship, he was now given an opportunity to live a new life and that is living out of his born again self.

There is No Final Condemnation Under the Gospel

The Bible says in Romans 8:1, "Therefore, [there is] now no condemnation [no adjudging guilty of wrong] for those who are in Christ Jesus, who live [and] walk not after the dictates of the flesh, but after the dictates of the Spirit" (AMP).[13]

The flesh represents the law. The law in itself cannot deliver us from sin. That deliverance comes from the Gospel alone. Romans 7:23–25 says, "But I see another law in my members, warring against the law of my mind, and bringing me into captivity to the law of sin, which is in my members."

This implies that there is condemnation under the law, and would continue to be if not for the Gospel of Jesus Christ. No condemnation does not mean that the sin of believers is not to be condemned just as it is for anyone else. No condemnation is taught in the scriptures; the Gospel does not pronounce condemnation as does the law. Its function is to pardon; the function of the law is to condemn. The law never affords deliverance, but always condemns; the object of the Gospel is to free us from condemnation and to set the soul at liberty. Christ paid the price for our sins.

There is no final condemnation under the Gospel. The function, design, and tendency of the Gospel is to free us from the condemning sentence of the law. This is its first glorious announcement: that it frees lost and ruined sinners from a most fearful and terrible condemnation.

We have to choose whether or not we are going to live our lives after the spirit of Christ. We have been given a new nature and a new spirit; we are a new creation—the born again. Walking in the spirit is walking in our born again self by consciously choosing, by faith, to rely on the Holy Spirit to guide in thought, word, and deed. Failure to rely on the Holy Spirit's guidance will result in a believer not living up to the calling and standing that the new nature (the born again self) provides.

Romans 8:2 "For the law of the Spirit of life in Christ Jesus hath made me free from the law of sin and death."

The Spirit of life is the Holy Spirit. He was present at the creation of the world (Genesis 1:2), and He is the power behind the rebirth of every born again Christian. He gives us the power to live out of our born again self. The Spirit of life in Christ Jesus has made the born again person free from the law of sin and death.

"With the arrival of Jesus, the Messiah, that fateful dilemma is resolved. Those who enter into Christ's being-here-for-us no longer have to live under a continuous, low-lying black cloud. A new power is in operation. The Spirit of Life in Christ, like a strong wind, has magnificently cleared the air, freeing you from a fated lifetime of brutal tyranny at the hands of sin and death."[14]

I Am a Good Person; I recite my Rosary and Made My Sacraments

Here is a demonstration of the law of sin and death. One day, I was sharing with a former coworker of mine, who is Catholic. I said to him, "If you were to die tonight and stand before God, and He was to ask you why he should let you into heaven, what would you say?"

He replied, "I am a good person; I recite my rosary and made my sacraments."

I said to him, "You say that you are a good person, and you are according to the world's standards. However, even as a good person, would you say that you sin according to God's laws (there are 613 laws cited in the Old Testament) at least once a day? Maybe a little lie, maybe you thought something evil about your coworker or boss, or maybe you looked at a woman with lust in your eyes?"

"Yes, probably more than once a day."

Well as a good person, at one sin a day... that would come out to be 365 sins a year, and you are forty-five years old, so let's calculate that from the age of twelve... That means you have sinned at least 16,425 times as a good person; twice a day would be 32,850 times, and you still would be a good person. Now if you were in a court of law standing in front of a judge with 32,850 violations, what would you think he would do?"

"Throw me into jail."

"Yes, that's right, because the law requires justice, and justice requires punishment. The breaking of the law brings condemnation."

Trying to live by some type of rituals or regulations will always bring failure and guilt. I like what Eugene H. Peterson says from *The Message: The Bible in Contemporary Language*, it states: "Those who think they can do it on their own end up obsessed with measuring their own moral muscle but never get around to exercising it in real life. Those who trust God's action in them find that God's Spirit is in them – living and breathing God! Obsession with self in these matters is a dead end; attention to God leads us out into the open, into a spacious, free life. Focusing on the self is the opposition of focusing on God. Anyone completely absorbed in self ignores God, ends up thinking more about self than God. That person ignores who God is and what he is doing. And God isn't pleased at being ignored" (Roman 8:5-8).

All the good works that we do that comes from self is nothing but dead works, because it is all based on performance. Dead works bring nothing but condemnation.

> "It stands to reason, doesn't it, that if the alive-and-present God who raised Jesus from the dead moves into your life, he'll do the same thing in you that he

40

did in Jesus, bringing you alive to himself? When God lives and breathes in you (and he does, as surely as he did in Jesus), you are delivered from that dead life. With his Spirit living in you, your body will be as alive as Christ's!" (Romans 8:11 The Message: The Bible in Contemporary Language).

Living out of your born again self is allowing God to live in you and through you. Recognizing that even though you still experience all the limitations of sin, yet you still experience life on God's terms.

Justice Cried Out, "Punishment and Death"

Romans 6:23 says, "The wages of sin is death; but the gift of God is eternal life through Jesus Christ our Lord." Jesus Christ came to fulfill all the requirements of the law. The law required justice, and justice cried out, "punishment and death!"

The Old Testament gives us a picture of the law. If anyone broke the law, they had to be subjected to some kind of punishment or death. There had to be a day of atonement. The Old Testament atonement was only a shadow of what was to come.

Who will pay the price for sin? There is no remission of sin apart of the shedding of blood. There must be a day of atonement. In Exodus 30:10, we read that once every year, the high priest alone would enter into the Holy of Holies. On the great day of atonement, he entered the Holy of Holies, first to burn incense, (Leviticus 16:12), and then to sprinkle the blood of the bullock on the mercy seat (Leviticus 16:1417). Then he was to kill the goat of the sin offering and bring the blood within the veil to sprinkle it on the mercy seat. The blood of the bullock was offered for himself and his household—thus keeping it impressed upon his own mind and the mind of the people the fact that they are all sinners. The blood of the goat was offered for the sins of the people (Leviticus 16:15). The object was to make expiation for all the sins of the people once a year. The repetition of these sacrifices was a constant remembrance of sin, and the design was that neither the priests nor the people should lose sight of the fact that they were violators of God's law.

> Hebrews 9: 12–14 "Neither by the blood of goats and calves, but by his own blood he entered in once into the holy place, having obtained eternal redemption for us. For if the blood of bulls and goats, and the ashes of an heifer sprinkling the unclean, sanctifieth to the purifying of the flesh: How much more shall the blood of Christ, who through the eternal Spirit offered himself without spot to God, purge your conscience from dead works to serve the living God?"

God would not be a God of justice if sin was not punished. The Old Testament sacrifice was only a shadow of the reality of what was to come. When Jesus came he became our high priest of the new covenant, he bypassed the earthly tabernacle and went straight to the holy place in heaven. He also bypassed the sacrifices consisting of animal blood and other rituals of purification which were only temporary in solving the sin problem. Therefore, only the blood of Jesus can clean us of our sins. Jesus freed us from the law of sin and death as he offered himself as an unblemished sacrifice. The old plan required a sacrificial death to set salvation in motion. So Moses who was type of Christ read all of the terms of the plan of the law of God. Therefore, he took the blood of the sacrificed animals and sprinkled the blood on the mercy seat and said, "This is the blood of the covenant commanded by God."

Practically everything in a will hinges on a death. That's why blood, the evidence of death, is used so much in our tradition, especially regarding forgiveness of sins.

Praise be to God, justice has been served, Jesus who was innocent, who knew no sin, was beaten with 39 stripes, nailed to the cross and crucify. However, that is not the end, for on the third day he was raised up and he entered into the holies of holies in heaven and offered himself to God as the sacrifice for our sins. This sacrifice was once and for all, summing up all the other sacrifices in this sacrifice of himself, the final solution of sin.

My Former Coworker Did Not Realize that He Was Suffering from a Disease Called Leprosy (Sin)

Luke 5:12–16 talks about a man who, upon seeing Jesus, fell on his face and begged him, saying, "Lord, if thou wilt, thou canst make me clean." This man, unlike some, knew that he needed to be changed, for he was a leper.

Among the Jews, several skin diseases were classified as leprosy. One form of leprosy attacks the nerves so that the victim cannot feel pain. Infection easily sets in, and this leads to degeneration of the tissues. The limb becomes deformed and eventually falls off. It was the task of the Jewish priests to examine people to determine whether they were lepers (see Leviticus 13). Infected people were isolated and could not return to normal society until declared "cleansed." Leprosy was used by Isaiah as a picture of sin (see Isaiah 1:4–6).

Like sin, leprosy is deeper than the skin and cannot be helped by mere surface measures. Also like sin, leprosy spreads, and as it spreads, it defiles. As previously mentioned, when leprosy attacks the nerves, you cannot feel the pain—so it is with sin. My former coworker did not realize that he was suffering from this disease.

> Isaiah 1:4, 6 says, "Ah sinful nation, a people laden with iniquity, a seed of evildoers, children that are corrupters...From the sole of the foot even unto the head there is no soundness in it; but wounds, and bruises, and putrefying sores: they have not been closed, neither bound up, neither mollified with ointment."

The man who begged Jesus not only needed to be changed, but he wanted to be changed. Lepers were required to keep their distance, but he was so determined that he broke the law and approached the Lord Jesus personally. By the grace and power of God, this man was changed! In fact, Jesus even touched the man, which meant that Jesus, according to the Jewish law, became unclean himself. This is a beautiful picture of what Jesus has done for lost sinners: he becomes sin for us that we might be made clean.

My former co-worker did not realize that he was suffering from the sin of self-righteousness. What happens when somebody is self-righteous is they are comparing themselves to others and measuring themselves as a better keeper of the rules. A self-righteous person will become irate. Their identity is wrapped in the false idea they are not as much a sinner as someone else. Self-righteous is a sin, it is like leprosy, it will get so entrenched in us that we will no longer realize the pain of this disease.

Thank God we, those who are born again, have been made clean. We have been touched by the master. No longer are we walking around and living with this disease that leads to death, called sin. We have been set free.

Living Out of Your Born Again Self has Nothing to Do with Performance

Jesus Christ paid it all—we are set free. Hebrews 12:2 says, "Who for the joy that was set before him endured the cross."

Living out of the born again self is not about performance; it is about a love relationship with our Lord and Savior Jesus Christ. The love of the Lord was so great that it brought him joy to endure the cross; my God, what a love! In your born again self, there is nothing but the love of God. For God so loved us that He saved us. As we love Him out of the born again self, we automatically want to please him, not ourselves. God lives in us and gives us the power, by His love, to live for him. Our life no longer belongs to us; we have been bought with a price, and love was that price. 1 Corinthians 6:20 says, "For you were bought at a price: therefore glorify God in your body, and in your spirit, which are God's."

Living out of your born again self has nothing to do with performance, just love. If you have a problem with continuous sinning, then you really have a love problem. I had a problem with my flesh. I wanted to please my flesh. Pleasing the flesh will always lead to sin. I had to confess to God and myself that I loved my flesh and wanted to please it. The love of my flesh was hindering my love for God. It was not until I came into the reality of Galatians 2:20 that:

> "I am [that is, my false identity self, my flesh] crucified with Christ: [all of my sins past, present, future were nailed to the cross], nevertheless I [my born again self] live; yet not I, [that is my false identity] but Christ lives in me:[born again self] and the life [the zoë, God-kind of life] which I [my born again self] now live in the flesh [because I have died to self-] I live by faith of the Son of God, who loved me, [when I was dead in sin Christ died for you and me] and gave himself for me" (Galatians 2:20, emphasis added).

We must remind ourselves that our life is not about performance. We have made a decision to give up our old life. Our old lives have been crushed and it was a painful process. We are no longer living our old life. No Christ's life is showing us how and enabling us to live this new life. We have made a decision to completely identify with him. Our ego is no longer central. It is no longer important that we appear righteous before you or have your good opinion. We are no longer driven to impress God, why because Christ lives in us. This life that we are living in the flesh is not ours, but we live it by faith in the Son of God, who loved us even when we were in sin: He gave himself for us.

I have realized that this new life is all about the love of God and not us. It is about living in love with Christ and maturing into our true selves, being born again.

How do we live out of the born again self?
By putting off our false identity self
Ephesians 4:22, "That ye put off concerning the former conversation the old man, which is corrupt according to the deceitful lusts."

By having a new mind-set
Ephesians 4:23, "And be renewed in the spirit of your mind."

By putting on a new self
Ephesians 4:24, "And that you put on the new man, which after God is created in righteousness and true holiness."

By walking in the light as the born again
Ephesians 5:8, "For you were once darkness, but now you are light in the Lord. Walk as children of light" (NKJV).

By making every effort to live out of your born again self
Second Peter 1:4-8, "Through these he has given us his very great and precious promises, so that through them you may participate in the divine nature and escape the corruption in the world caused by evil desires. For this very reason, make every effort to add to your faith goodness; and to goodness, knowledge; and to knowledge, self-control; and to self-control, perseverance and to perseverance, godliness; and to godliness,

brotherly kindness; and to brotherly kindness, love. For if you possess these qualities in increasing measure, they will keep you from bring ineffective and unproductive in your knowledge of our Lord Jesus Christ" (NIV).

By helping other to do the same
Hebrews 10:24, "And let us consider one another in order to stir up love and good works" (NKJV).

By not forsaking the house of God
Hebrews 10:25, "Not forsaking the assembling of ourselves together, as in the manner of some, but exhorting one another, and so much the more as you see the Day approaching" (NKJV).

In our born again self we have everything we need to live this life for Christ. Christ the hope of glory lives in us, the born again.

> John 15:4-7, "Abide in me, and I in you. As the branch cannot bear fruit of itself except it abide in the vine; no more can ye, except ye abide in me. I am the vine, and ye are the branches: He that abideth in me, and I in him, the same bringeth forth much fruit: for without me ye can do nothing. If a man abide not in me, he is cast forth as a branch, and is withered; and men gather them, and cast them into the fire, and they are burned. If ye abide in me, and my word abide in you, ye shall ask what ye will, and it shall be done unto you."

His Life Will Flow Through Us and Be Demonstrated Through Our Thoughts, Our Conversations, and Our Actions

The Word of God reminds us that apart from abiding in Him, we cannot do anything to please God. Since our life is now connected and directed by God, it is necessary to know how to live out of this connection (I call it the born again connection) and receive the benefits that God intends for us. That is living victoriously. As we abide in him, his life will flow through us and be demonstrated through our thoughts, our conversations, and our actions.

The Bible says in John15:4, "Abide in me, and I in you. As the branch cannot bear fruit of itself, except it abide in the vine; no more can ye, except it abide in the vine; no more can ye, except ye abide in me."

To abide means to stay in a given place, state, relation or expectancy. It also means to continue, endure, be present, remain, stand and tarry.

This command is really an invitation to a deeper love relationship with God and greater victory in life. Christ tells us to live in Him. He gives us an invitation to make our home in Him. He reminds us that, He is living in us. In the same way that a branch can't bear fruit by itself but only by being joined to the vine; so it is we can't bear fruit unless we are joined to Him.

This is also an inroad to godly living. The key to living this life of Christ, the born again life is that abiding gives you the power to live it. You must go right to the source of your power, every day in every way. Abiding means continually staying in an attitude of prayer, praising Him continually, and always asking Him to favor you with His will through wisdom and revelation.

Remember the master's words: "For without me ye can do nothing" (John 15:5). Separated, we can't produce a thing. Christ goes on to say: "If a man abide not in me, he is cast forth as a branch, and is withered; and men gather them, and cast them into the fire, and they are burned" (John 15:6). Anyone who is not abiding in the Master is like dead wood, soon to be gathered up and thrown into the fire. If we continue to make are home in Him, then we can be sure that whatever we ask will be listened to and acted upon. John 15:7 says, "If ye abide in me, and my words abide in you, ye shall ask what ye will, and it shall be done unto you." Remember: it is impossible to live out of your born again self without abiding in Christ.

When you begin to make a decision to live out of your born again self, you will begin to see tangible results. You will become the salt of the earth, and you will become a light in dark places. Even the people around you will have to begin to change.

You are a Grown Man Crying Like a Baby. Do You Know What You Need?

I remember in my former job, I was having some severe problems with one man in my crew. He knew that I was a believer, and he fought against me. One day I could not help myself, and I was sharing with him about the love of Jesus. He abruptly said to me, "I do not want to hear anything about your Jesus. You can take your Jesus and [expletive] just keep your mouth shut about your Jesus! All I want to hear from you is whatever instructions you have for the job assignment." I replied, "Yes, sir." That night, I went to bed with that lost soul on my spirit. Well, as usual, the Holy Spirit woke me up at 4:00 a.m. to spend some time with him. In my prayer time, the Spirit instructed me to go into work one hour early, anoint the seats in the work truck with oil, and pray over the truck as well as against the spirit of unbelief. For one week, I went in as instructed, anointed the seats, and prayed. The next week, my coworker came to work, got into the truck, and began to tell me all of his personal problems. Monday, Tuesday, Wednesday, Thursday, and by Friday, he began to cry. I gave him some tissues and said, "You are a grown man crying like a baby, now blow your nose." I continued and said, "Do you know what you need?" He replied, while sniffing and wiping his nose, "What do I need?" I replied, "You need Jesus!" That day, he became born again.

Praise God! Hallelujah!

I am talking about how to live out of your born again self. The love of God in you will cause a river to flow out of your inmost being; it's called the river of love, a river that overflows. This river in your born again self cannot be contained. That is what happened to my coworker. He got caught up in the river's current and it was called God's love. The current of the river swept him into the loving arms of the master.

We Were God's Enemies, But We Are Now His Friends

That is why God has given the born again the ministry of reconciliation. "And all things are of God, who hath reconciled us to himself by Jesus Christ, and hath given to us the ministry of reconciliation" (2 Corinthians 5:18). Our assignment is to reconcile man to God and man to man. Webster's 1828 English Dictionary defines the word "reconciliation" as:

1.) The act of reconciling parties at variance; renewal of friendship after disagreement or enmity.

2.) In scripture, the means by which sinners are reconciled and brought into a state of favor with God, after natural estrangement or enmity; the atonement; expiation.

3.) Agreement of things seemingly opposite, different or inconsistent.

I was operating in the ministry of reconciliation in the above example with my former coworker. He was a sinner, thus, out of relationship with God. I was once a sinner and had no power or authority to bring anyone back to a relationship with God. However, because of my born again experience, I was given the power and authority to minister reconciliation to my former coworker, who was living in a broken relationship with God. This power and authority is given to all those who are born again. All this is from God, who reconciled us to himself through Christ and gave us this ministry of reconciliation. God reconciled the world to himself in Christ, not counting men's sins against them.

The Bible says that Christ reconciled us to God: "When we were enemies, we were reconciled to God by the death of his son..." (Romans 5:10). The fact that we were enemies of God means that our relationship with him was broken.

When Christ died on the cross, he satisfied God's judgment and made it possible for God's enemies to find peace with him. Our reconciliation to God involves the acceptance of this free gift of grace and the forgiveness of our sins. The result of Jesus' sacrifice is that our relationship has changed from enmity to friendship. The Bible says, "No longer do I call you slaves, for the slave does not know what his master is doing; but I have called you friends" (John 15:15 NASU).[15] The Bible's definition of reconciliation is a glorious truth! We were God's enemies, but are now his friends. We were in a state of condemnation because of our sins, but we are now forgiven. We are the born again.

Living out of your born again self is to understand that God is our creator, and He has given us a manual to live by. If we want to live a victorious life in Christ by living out of our born again self, then we are going to have to follow the instructions in the manual. Our manual is the Holy Bible. We must be serious about living this new resurrection life with Christ—pursuing

Godly ways with the mind of Christ, seeing things from his perspective, and understanding that our old life has died and that our new life (our born again self) is hidden with Christ.

Below are some instructions to follow from our manual (the Holy Bible):

The Old Man versus The New Man
Colossians 3:5
Put to death what is earthly in you:
> Sexual immorality
> Uncleanness
> Inordinate affection
> Evil desire
> Covetousness, which is idolatry

Colossians 3:8–9
Put off all of the following:
> Anger
> Wrath
> Malice
> Slander
> Filth
> Obscene talk
> Lying

Colossians 3:9
See that you have put off the old man with his practices (your false-identity self)...

Colossians 3:10, 12, 13
...And have put on the new man (the born again self), displaying the following:
> Renewed knowledge (the new creation)

After the image of the Creator
Put on holiness (the born again self)
Compassion
Kindness
Humbleness of mind
Meekness
Longsuffering
Forbearing one another
Forgiving one another

Colossians 3:14–17
And above all things, the following should be done:

> Put on love, which is the bond of perfection.
>
> Let the peace of God rule in your heart (your born again self).
>
> Let the word of Christ dwell in you (your born again self) richly.
>
> In all wisdom, teaching, and admonishing (to reprove gently but earnestly), be able to counsel (another) against something to be avoided. To remind yourself of something forgotten or disregarded, as an obligation or a responsibility.
>
> Give God praise in songs and in your heart.
>
> Do everything in the name of the Lord Jesus.
>
> Give thanks to God.

Know This: The Old Man is Crucified

"Knowing this, that our old man is crucified with him, that the body of sin might be destroyed, that henceforth we should not serve sin" (Romans 6:6).

All Christians are supposed to know this. This illustrates the fact that by Christ's crucifixion, our corrupt nature has been crucified, or put to death, also, and that we should be free from the slavery of sin.

"Our old man;" Paul uses this expression to illustrate our sinful and corrupt nature—the passions and evil propensities that exist before the heart is renewed. It refers to the love of sin and the indulgence of sinful propensities in opposition to the new disposition, which exists after the soul, is converted. This conversion is called "the new man."

"Is crucified;" This means put to death, as if on a cross. In this expression, there is a personification of the corrupt propensities of our nature represented as "our old man," our native disposition. The figure is here carried out and this old man, this corrupt nature, is represented as having been put to death in an agonizing and torturous manner. The pains of crucifixion were perhaps the most torturous. Death in this manner was lingering and distressing. Apostle Paul uses this expression "is crucified" to refer to the painful and protracted struggle that everyone goes through when evil propensities are subdued, when the corrupt nature is slain, and when a converted sinner gives him- or herself up to God. Sin dies within the believer, and he or she becomes dead to the world and to sin.

All who have been born again can relate to this description. The born again remembers the anguish of conviction, the struggle of corrupt passion for the ascendancy, the dying convulsions of sin in the heart, the long lingering conflict before it was subdued, and when the soul became submissive to God. Nothing can express this better than the cross of Jesus.[16]

However, you still carry around the old man; the old man is your flesh, or physical body, which has a carnal mind. Your physical body has lusts and desires. Your body can produce thoughts and imaginings. The scripture says "the works of the flesh are manifest, which are these: adultery fornication, uncleanness, lasciviousness, idolatry, witchcraft..." (Galatians 5:19–21).

I did not say that you still carry around your old nature. Your former unregenerate spirit is your old nature. Remember 2 Corinthians 5: 17: "Therefore, if any man be in Christ, he is a new creature, old things are passed away, behold, all things are become new." So behold, what is new? It is the new man, the born again self; the new man is your inward man; he is a new creature. It is a spiritual mind that pays attention to the things of God.

When a person is born again, he is spiritually circumcised, and the body of the sins of the flesh is separated from the soul and spirit of man. Colossians 2:11–13 says, "In whom also ye are circumcised with the circumcision made without hands, in putting off the body of the sins of the flesh by the circumcision of Christ."

The old man (your flesh) was put off at your spiritual circumcision by the Lord, using the Word of God. It is dead as far as God is concerned, and it is dead in the sense of its power and authority over you. The reason why you still sin is because of your flesh/ body/ old man and because you allow your body to fulfill the lusts it has.

What is More Beautiful: An Airplane Landing or an Airplane Taking Off?

The Lord gave me an illustration of the Old Man versus the New Man. One night while teaching Bible study on this subject, I asked the question, "What is more beautiful, an airplane landing or an airplane taking off?" Some said landing because they are safe on the ground. Some said taking off because it will take them to their destination. I asked that question not because there was a right or wrong answer, but because I wanted them to see the law that is in place. To me, the airplane taking off is more beautiful. I began working for Pan American Airways in 1968 and saw many airplanes take off— and what a beautiful sight. Now look in your mind's eye and see the airplane taking off down the runway as it builds up momentum, as it lifts off the ground, and begins to soar. The amazing thing is that while the plane is building momentum, the law of gravity is present all around, trying to keep the plane on the ground, but another law comes into effect that lifts that aircraft off the ground and pulls it upward, defying the law of gravity. That law is called aerodynamics.

The law of aerodynamics has always been present, even before it was understood and used to develop airplanes for flight. Every law, whether it is the Law of Moses or Newton's law, was placed there by God to teach us the truth about our reality. The Word of God says in Colossians 1:16:

> "For by him were all things created, that are in heaven, and that are in earth, visible and invisible, whether they be thrones, or dominions, or principalities or powers: all things were created by him and for him. He is before all things and by him all things consist."

Paul stated this same principle in Romans 7:22–23:

> "For I delight in the law of God after the inward man: But I see another law in my members, warring against the law of my mind, and bringing me into captivity to the law of sin, which is in my members."

The law of sin and death was not always present. As you read earlier, God created man in his image and likeness. Man was in perfect harmony with God; there was no sin or death until the fall of Adam. As a result, the law of sin and death (our "law of gravity" or sin nature) was introduced. When we were in our old nature (sin nature) we had no power to overcome the gravitational pull of sin. It took a higher law (God's love) to free us from the bondage of sin and death. What made us (the born again self) free? The answer is "the law of the Spirit of life in Christ Jesus has made me free from the law of sin and death" (Romans 8:2).

We are a Type of Boeing 747 Called Born Again

Now, when I worked for Pan American Airways, I was amazed at the size of the Boeing 747 aircraft. It could carry four hundred passengers. It wing span was 195 feet, 8 inches, its length was 231 feet, 10 inches, and its weight was 735,000 pounds—a gigantic plane for its time. It seemed almost too big to fly. Skeptics predicted catastrophic crashes, crumpled runways, and gridlocked passenger terminals. It was the largest commercial plane at the time. It looked impossible to overcome the law of gravity. But with its powerful engines combined with the law of aerodynamics, the plane was able to lift itself off the ground, defying gravity, traveling at a rate of 640 miles per hour; breaking free from the bonds of the earth as it lifted itself 35,000 feet above the Earth's atmosphere. Since 1970, the Boeing 747 has flown more than 3.5 billion passengers—the equivalent of more than half the world's population.

If the natural man can defy the law of gravity and raise itself above the earth, how much more you and I, those who are born again?

We are a type of Boeing 747 called 'Born Again'. We have been created and chosen in Christ from the foundation of the world. We entered a realm that we thought was our real world and saw ourselves as a human being separated from God, but thanks be to God because our life is in Christ allows us to rise above the law of sin and death. We cannot let the old way of thinking (the old man) keep us locked into the gravitational pull of the earth (satisfying the desires of the flesh).

When an Airplane Crashes, the First Thing They Look for is the Black Box

Your old man (your flesh, your old way of thinking) will always try to keep you from living out of your born again self. If you do not know how to live out of your born again self, then you may experience a crash. This crash will not cause you to lose your salvation. However, it will cause you to fall back to the surface of the ground, and you will be living beneath your born again privileges as a child of God.

When an airplane crashes, the first thing they look for is the black box. What is a black box? It is a voice recorder and a flight data recorder. While they do nothing to help the plane when it is in the air, both these pieces of equipment are vitally important should the plane crash. For they help crash investigators find out what happened before the crash. It is called the black box because the data of what caused the plane to crash is hidden in it. The black box is not actually black, but bright orange. It is called the black box because it holds the mystery of the crash.

We Have a Black Box. It's Called the Carnal Mind

Similarly we too have a black box. It's called the carnal mind. Romans 8:7 says, "Because the carnal mind is enmity against God: for it is not subject to the law of God, neither indeed can be. So then they that are in the flesh cannot please God." Locked in our mind is our past memories; everything we did before we were born again is stored in our mind. The enemy wants to remind us of what we used to do or what we did one hour ago that did not please God.

One day, this lady came up to me and said, "I remember when you were in a fight and..." She began to explain some bad things that I did. I replied, "I never did anything like that. That was my old life, my old nature. I am born again, a new man in Christ. I, my new self, never did that." The Devil always wants to remind you of your old self.

I know a woman who is born again and loves God. However, she has fixed in her mind that she will never overcome the lust of her flesh. She was molested as a little girl by her uncle, and he taught her how to have sex. She told me that she enjoyed sex and learned how to please men. She said this knowledge empowered her to manipulate men. She married and was very much in love with her husband. However, the lust of her flesh always wanted more sex—so much that she started having sex with many men outside of her marriage. It was not until after many years that she learned how to die to self and live as a new creature in Christ and was able to live a victorious life in Christ.

In This Black Box are Old Memories, and Many of These Memories are Toxic

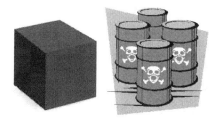

This woman, as well as many other women or men with different problems, need to locate their black box. Inside this black box is stored old memories, and many of these memories are toxic. These toxic memories are poisonous thoughts that trigger negative and anxious emotions, which produce biochemicals. In fact, according to neuroscientists, for every memory you make, you have a corresponding emotion attached to it, which is stored in your brain and as a photocopy in your body's cells. We all need to take authority over our past memories and know that God has given us a new nature. The old nature has been crucified; we have to be willing to nail it to the cross. The Bible says in Romans 8:13, "For if ye live after the flesh, ye shall die: but if ye through the Spirit do mortify the deeds of the body, ye shall live."

Our bodies were birthed out of a sinful nature, it is dying. It only wants to please itself. The life purchased and promised does not immortalize the body in its present state. Our bodies are appointed to die; it is under a sentence of death. Therefore, we have to make a decision that we will no longer live by the dictates of our flesh. We have to renew our minds, because our minds are full of old memories that are toxic. If we use our lives to do what we want, we will die spiritually. But the life of the Holy Spirit in us (our born again spirit) will strengthen us to put to dead those old memories and toxic thoughts and inclinations. His life in us will cause us to live a born again life in Him, and our lives will be lived to the glory of God.

Our Inner Man (the Born Again) Must be Released

Romans 7:22 says, "For I delight in the law of God according to the inner man" (NKJV). Ephesians 3:16 says, "To be strengthened with might through His Spirit in the inner man [the born again]" (NKJV) Paul also said in 2 Corinthians 4:16, "Even though our outward man is perishing, yet the inward man is being renewed day by day" (NKJV).

The Bible divides our being into the outer man (flesh) and the inner man (the born again). God resides in the inner man, and the man outside this God-occupied inner man is the outer man (your flesh). God has placed Himself, His Spirit, His life, and His power in us. In order for Christians to live for God, our inner man must be released, and the flesh must be broken.

The fundamental problem with many Christians is that their inner man cannot break out of their outer man. We have to know that the first obstacle of living out of our born again selves is ourselves, not other things. If our inner man is an imprisoned, confined man, then our born again selves are hindered and not easily released.

Living out of the born again self depends on whether we allow the master to dismantle our outer man in order to make way for our inner man. As soon as the inner man is released, many sinners will be blessed, and many Christians will receive grace. How can we cause this breaking of the outer man and the releasing of the inner man? By mortifying the deeds of the body.

Mortify the Deeds of the Body

What does the word "mortify" mean and how do we mortify the deeds of the body?

Mortify, or mortification, has several meanings in English. The first is to feel ashamed or embarrassed. The second meaning is to subdue the body (or its needs and desires) through self-denial and discipline. The word mortify comes from the Latin word *mortificare*, which means "to kill or subdue." We get our English words "mortuary" and "mortician" from this Latin root. Therefore, to mortify the deeds of the flesh means to "kill" the sins of the flesh.

Romans 8:13 says, "For if ye live after the flesh, ye shall die: but if ye through the Spirit do mortify the deeds of the body, ye shall live." Our new nature, which is the born again self, has been given by the Holy Spirit the power to subdue the flesh. Colossians 3:5 says, "Mortify therefore your members, which are upon the earth; fornication, uncleanness, inordinate affection, evil concupiscence, and covetousness, which is idolatry."

Christ took care of the sin nature on the cross when he said, "It is finished" (John 19:30). It is the responsibility of the believer to embrace this reality that the sin nature has been put to death. We must remind our flesh (the old man) that it has been put to death; it has been nailed to the cross.

In Romans 8:13, Paul is making a contrast between believers (the born again) and nonbelievers. Nonbelievers are those who live according to the flesh. By contrast, believers (the born again) are those who, by the Spirit, put to death the deeds of the body. To live according to the flesh is to have your mind set on the flesh and to have a mind that is hostile to God and does not submit to his law. To live according to the flesh is to continue living according to the sinful nature that does not obey God. This is the life of an unbeliever. The person who lives his life according to the flesh will die. This is not speaking of physical death because that is a fate that all people will face as a result of sin. Paul is speaking of eternal death in hell.

My Flesh is Dead Toward Marijuana. What is Your Flesh Dead Toward?

The born again makes a decision, by the power of the Spirit, to put to death the deeds of the body. In other words, through the working of God's Holy Spirit, who only dwells in the born again, the believer engages in the process of sanctification, or growing in holiness. The believer, in contrast to the nonbeliever, has his mind set on the Spirit and submits to God's law. It is important for me to stop here and to say that the believer does sin. 1 John 1:8–10 says:

"If we say (the born again) that we have no sin, we deceive ourselves, and the truth is not in us. If we confess our sins, He is faithful and just to forgive us our sins, and to cleanse us from all unrighteousness. If we say that we have not sinned, we make him a liar, and his word is not in us" (emphasis added).

However, the born again no longer possess a sin nature. Putting to death the deeds of the body is a continual process that the believer must engage in on a daily basis. Jesus said in Mark 8:34, "Whosoever will come after me, let him deny himself, and take up his cross, and follow me."

Many years ago, I loved to smoke marijuana. I smoked it every day. If someone came to me, placed it before me, my flesh would say yes, and I would smoke it. Now if someone came and placed a pound of marijuana before me, my flesh would not even move. Why? Because my flesh is dead toward marijuana. What is your flesh dead toward?

A friend of mind was suffering for over thirty years with alcohol and drug addiction. He was very active in the local church, and he confessed Christ as his Savior. However, he just was not willing to die to the flesh. His body was crazy for more and more poison. He told me that one night, he was lying in his bed and just felt like he was going to die, so he cried out to Jesus. He turned to his wife and asked her to take him to an alcohol and drug rehabilitation center. He said that he stayed there for four days and made a decision to make Jesus the Lord of his life. That was eight years ago, and he has not touched or craved any alcohol or drugs since. I asked him if he would have a desire to use if someone was to put alcohol and drugs in front of him. He said, "No, I would have no desire. It would not move me." His flesh is now dead toward alcohol and drugs.

What Does a Living Sacrifice Look Like?

The Bible tells us to present our bodies as a living sacrifice. Romans 12:1–2 says, "I beseech you, therefore, brethren, by the mercies of God, that ye present your bodies a living sacrifice, holy, acceptable unto God, which is your reasonable service." The Merriam Webster dictionary defines sacrifice as "the act of offering something to God." For those who are born again, the only acceptable worship is to offer ourselves completely to the Lord. Romans 12:1 say, "Holy, acceptable unto God, which is your reasonable service." In view of the ultimate sacrifice of Jesus for us, this is only our reasonable service unto Him. The passage goes on to say, "And be not conformed to this world: but be ye transformed by the renewing of your mind, that ye may prove what is that good, and acceptable, and perfect will of God" (Romans 12:2).

What does a living sacrifice look like in the practical sense? The Bible tells us, *"and be not conformed to this world."* So we are a living sacrifice by not conforming in this world. The world is defined for us in 1 John 2: 15–16, "The lust of the flesh, the lust of the eyes, and the pride of life." All that the world has to offer can be reduced to these three things. The lust of the flesh includes everything that appeals to our appetites, which involves excessive desires. Lust of the eyes mostly involves materialism, coveting whatever we see that we don't have and envying those who have what we want. The pride of life is defined by any ambition for that which puffs us up and puts us on the throne of our own lives.

We Must Change the Way We Think

Let go back to the black box. This black box, the carnal mind, is your old man. To live as the new man, you must live a in a state of always renewing your mind.

Romans 12:2 "And do not be conformed to this world, but be transformed by the renewing of your mind, that you may prove what is good and acceptable and perfect will of God" (NKJV). Another translation says, "Do not change yourselves to be like the people of this world, but be changed within by a new way of thinking" (NCV).[17]

To live out of the born again self, we must change the way we think. How do we change the way we think? By changing one thought at a time because thoughts influence every decision, word, action, and physical reaction we make. As the born again, we are a new creation. We are no longer a victim of our biology. God has given us a design of hope: we can renew our minds, change, and heal. Scientific eyes have discovered that we have amazing brains filled with real physical thoughts that you can control.[18]

The Bible says, "And now, dear brothers and sisters, one final thing. Fix your thoughts on what is true, and honorable, and right, and pure, and lovely and admirable. Think about things that are excellent and worthy of praise" (Philippians 4:8 NLT).[19] How do we think about things that are excellent and worthy? By being transformed by the renewing of our minds.

According to Strong's Greek Dictionary, the Greek word for transformed is *metamorphoo* (our word metamorphosis comes from this word), and it means to change into another form.

The definition of metamorphosis includes the following:
>Change of the form or nature of a thing or person into completely different one, by natural or supernatural means;
>A striking alteration in appearance, character, or circumstance.

>Synonyms—changeover, conversion, transfiguration, transformation
>Related words—shift, transitory, adjustment, alteration, modification, reconstruction, reconversion, redoing, refashioning, reformation, remaking, remodeling, revamping, revision, reworking.[20]

All of the above words describe the transformation of the born again. If you are born again, there should be some evidence of change.

There was a Metamorphosis... He Saw a New Conversion, a New Appearance, a New Character, and a Transformation. He Saw the Born Again.

I remember that right after being born again, I flew back from Texas to New Jersey. I walked into the supermarket to pick up a few items. Suddenly this Muslim brother walks up to me and said, "As-salam-alaykum (peace be upon you), Brother Hasan." My legal name at that time was Khalif Majid Hasan. I replied, "wa alaykumu s-salam" (unto you be peace). He said, "Brother Hasan, something looks different about you. I see a glow around you. What happened to you?" I replied, "I have accepted Jesus Christ as my Savior. I am now a Christian." He just could not believe what he was seeing and hearing. So he encouraged me to come back to the mosque. After all, I was an Imam in the Islamic community. The next day was a day I have known for many years as Jummah (known as Friday congregational prayer). I entered into the mosque and greeted all of my Muslim brothers, and then sat down on the floor and began to listen to the *khutba* (sermon) about Jesus being only a prophet and how Prophet Muhammad was the last and greatest prophet. After the *khutba*, it was time for everyone to stand up for congregational prayer. I remained seated; my Muslim friend was astonished that I remained seated. He looked at me and said, "What are you doing? Stand up, and worship, and pray to Allah." I said to him kindly, "I am now a Christian; I cannot stand and pray."

There was a metamorphosis that this Muslim was seeing. He saw a new conversion, a new appearance, a new character, and a transformation. He saw the born again.

Maybe the above story is not your story. However, there should be some manifestation that you have been born again. What changeover, what character, what striking alternation, what refashioning, what metamorphosis has occurred in your life?

Are you truly born again? If so, then the reality of Romans 12:2 is being manifested in you. "Be transformed by the renewing of your mind" refers to a complete change of nature that occurs when our minds come into agreement with the truth of God's Word. As Jesus was transfigured in Matthew 17:2 so are we transformed to reflect God's glory as our hearts and spirits come into agreement with God's Word.

You and I must realize there is an intense warfare in our minds to come into agreement with either God or the Devil. That day when I was in the mosque, the Muslims tried to tell me that I was being deceived. They tried to change my mind about Christ. But my old nature was dead nailed to the cross. The Muslim brothers were very angry with me and said, "You came in here and disrespected our mosque. Do not come back. You are not welcome."

I am the born again, a new creation. Old things have passed away and behold, all things have become new. God has given us a new created spirit. However, we have the same old mind. Therefore, it is our responsibility to change the way we think by renewing our minds. If we change the way we think, then our feeling will change. A renewed mind not only thinks different thoughts, but also thinks from God's perspective. The truth of God's word is now our nature. We are made into God's image, and our words and thoughts have creative power to change our physical and spiritual circumstances. After all, God spoke the world into existence, and as the born again, we are carriers of God's glory.

Proverbs 23:87 says, "For as he thinketh in his heart, so is he." Our innermost thoughts are important in that they actually set the course of our lives. Carnal thinking, or our old way of thinking, reflects our fallen nature, which is incapable of comprehending the things of God or coming into agreement with God's Word.

The Heart

The Word of God is true. What does "For as he thinketh in his heart, so is he" mean? Neurologically your heart is sensitive to what you think and feel. Your thoughts directly affect your heart. Your heart is not just a pump. It is actually like another brain (and you thought you only had one brain). Science demonstrates that your heart has its own independent nervous system; it is referred to as 'the brain in the heart:'

Although previously unknown, neuroscientists have now discovered that there are at least 40,000 neurons (nerve cells) in the heart, as many as are found in various parts of the brain. In effect, the brain in your heart acts like a checking station for all the emotions generated by the flow of chemicals created by thoughts. The heart also produces an important biochemical substance called an atrial peptide (specifically ANF). It is the balance hormone that regulates many of your brain's functions and stimulates behavior.

New scientific evidence on the heart's neurological sensitivity indicates there are lines of communication between the brain and the heart that check the accuracy and integrity of your thought life. The reality is that your heart is in constant communication with your brain and the rest of your body.[21]

Wow! We are what we think.

Ephesians 4:30 says, "And grieve not the Holy Spirit of God, whereby ye are sealed unto the day of redemption."

The Holy Spirit is the third person of the God head. He lives in us; therefore, we can grieve Him by our thoughts because our thoughts affect our heart. What you think about expands and grows, taking on a life of its own. The direction this life takes could be good or bad; you get to choose.

Isaiah 7:15 says, "Butter and honey shall he eat, that he may know to refuse the evil, and choose the good."

What we choose to think about can foster joy, peace, and happiness or the complete opposite.

While writing this book, I was engaged in a conversation with a young man. He was feeling depressed because he was reflecting on his past—the memories of being molested as a little boy. He said to me, "You do not understand." I replied, "Young man, I do understand because I experienced the same thing." I began to share with him my experience of being molested as little boy. I could sense that I was getting emotional as I was remembering my past. I began to become aware of how I was feeling and how my body was reacting to my thoughts. I could feel a cascade of chemicals being activated and released by my remembering the event. Immediately I had to change the way I was thinking; as soon as I changed my thinking, my feelings changed.

Philippians 4:8 says, "And now, dear brothers and sisters, one final thing. Fix your thoughts on what is true, and honorable, and right, and pure, and lovely, and admirable. Think about things that are excellent and worthy of praise" (NLT).

To live out of your born again self you must understand 2 Corinthians 10:3–6:

> "For though we walk in the flesh, [our born-again self, lives in this flesh body] we do not war after the flesh:[do not fight the enemy from your old way of thinking] For the weapons of our warfare are not carnal, [our weapons are not the weapons the world uses] but mighty through God to the pulling down of strong holds; casting down imaginations, and every high thing that exalteth itself against the knowledge of God, and bringing into captivity every thought to the obedience of Christ. And having in a readiness to revenge all disobedience, when your obedience is fulfilled" (some emphasis added).

Summing all this up, we will do our best by filling our mind and meditating on things that will bring about this metamorphosis. By using our powerful God given tools, tearing down every imagination that try to erect itself against the truth of who God says we are. We must show the world that we have been transformed into the image that shows forth the glory of God.

I Am Now Engaged in a Battle Against the Enemy

As I write this and as you read this, we are engaged in a war. All kinds of thoughts are trying to enter into my mind. I am talking about ungodly, carnal inclinations. I am right now fighting, engaged in a battle against the enemy—and so are you by reading this book. We will be fighting this enemy as long as we are in this flesh. Why? Because our flesh is tied to this world and Satan is the prince of this world. John 14:30 says "For the prince of this world cometh." He is the prince and power of the air. Ephesians 2:2 says, "According to the prince of the power of the air."

Paul says in 2 Corinthians 10:4 "For the weapons of our warfare are not carnal, but mighty through God to pulling down of strong holds..."

What does Paul mean when he uses the word "warfare"? He is painting a picture for our mind that we are in a military campaign. We are soldiers in the army of God. The word "weapons" that Paul uses means the manner in which we fight; this manner is mighty.

"Mighty" in Greek is *dunatos*, which means, "powerful, capable, able."

Another form of "mighty" in Greek is *dumi*, which means; "prolonged" (will not go away).

And another form in Greek is *duo*, which means, "to go down or pull down."

The born again weapons of warfare are mighty, powerful, capable, able, and to pull down strongholds.

What Are Strongholds?

Stronghold comes from the Greek word "ochuroma," (Strong's Greek dictionary number 3794) which means, "to fortify, through the idea of holding something safely." A stronghold is like a castle or fortress.

- Spiritual strongholds are arguments, reasoning, and opinions that are contrary to the knowledge of Christ.
- Strongholds are from Satan and his host of demons.
- Strongholds are resilient; they require weapons to combat them.
- You cannot negotiate with a stronghold.
- Strongholds do not just go away with time.
- Strongholds must be destroyed, brought down, and demolished.

  2 Corinthians 10:5-6 says, "Casting down imaginations, and every high thing that exalteth itself against the knowledge of God, and bringing into captivity every thought to the obedience of Christ; and having in a readiness to revenge all disobedience, when your obedience is fulfilled."

What Are "Imaginations"?

The faculty of imagining, or of forming mental images or concepts of what is not actually present to the senses; the product of imagining a conception or mental creation, often a baseless or fanciful one.

Imagination is also called the faculty of imagining.

In the word "imagination," you will find the word "imagine." Remember: the Devil is always trying to give you ungodly thoughts and imaginations.

Casting Down Imaginations

No man has an original thought. Thoughts either come from God or the Devil. Thoughts from God we are not to cast down. However, all thoughts from the Devil are negative and prideful. We are to cast down the Devil's thoughts.

"And every high thing that exalted itself against the knowledge of God."
'Every high thing' refers to the proud and lofty thoughts from the Devil to men, which leads them to exalt themselves against the Gospel. All the pride of the human heart and of understanding is opposed to the knowledge of God.

"And bringing into captivity every thought to the obedience of Christ."
The figure here is taken from military conquests. The idea is that all the strongholds of unbelief, pride, and sin be demolished. When that is done, they should be thrown down, like the walls of a city. This also means that all the plans and purposes of the soul, the reason, the imagination, and all the

powers of the mind should be subdued or led in triumph by the Gospel, like the inhabitants of a captured city; therefore, this means to take every thought prisoner.

"And having in a readiness to revenge all disobedience..."
The born again is ready to fight the enemy of disobedience because he or she is clothed with power, aiming to subdue all things to Christ.

"When your obedience is fulfilled."
The kingdom of God can go forth in power in the born again when he or she is obedient to God. Others can be drawn to the Gospel by our obedience.

Fighting Against the Forces of Darkness

The born again knows that he or she is fighting against the forces of darkness. This is our reality: Our warfare is with the corrupt desires and sensual propensities of the heart, and with the remaining un-subdued propensities of our fallen nature (our flesh, the black box). Our warfare is with the power of darkness and the spirits of evil that seek to destroy us

(Ephesians 6:11-17; the prince of the air, our thoughts). Our war is against all sin in all its forms.

Thus our weapons are mighty and include the following:

W: Word of God; Ephesians 6:17: Hebrews 4:12
E: Effective prayer; James 5:16
A: Armor of God; Ephesians 6:13–17
P: Praises of God; 2 Chronicles 20:21–23
O: Offerings of God; Malachi 3:8–11
N: Name of God; Proverb 18:10
S: Spirit of God; Zechariah 4:6

Again, to live out of your born again self, you must know who you are fighting and what the weapons are at your disposal to defeat the enemy. I like what it says in The Message, the Bible in Contemporary Language:

> "God is strong, and he wants you strong. So take everything the Master has set out for you, well-made weapons of the best materials. And put then to use so you will be able to stand up to everything the Devil throws your way. This is no afternoon athletic contest that we'll walk away from and forget about in a couple of hours. This is for keeps, a life or deaths fight to the finish against the Devil and his angels.
>
> Be prepared. You're up against far more than you can handle on your own. Take all the help you can get, every weapon God has issued, so that when it's all over but the shouting you'll still be on your feet. Truth, righteousness, peace, faith, and salvation are more than words. Learn how to apply them. You'll

need them throughout your life. God's Word is an indispensable weapon. In the same way, prayer is essential in this on-going warfare. Pray hard and long. Pray for your brothers and sisters. Keep your eyes open. Keep each other's spirits up so that no one falls behind or drops out" (Ephesians 6: 10–18).

You and I cannot live out of the born again self any other way. Every day, we must apply the Word of God to our lives.

As a pastor, I get calls, text messages, or e-mails every day from those who are born again who just want to give up and feel that God just does not care about them. They will make statements like the following:

- *God really does not care about me.*
- *God does not love me.*
- *Why doesn't God help me?*
- *God is not blessing me.*

They are constantly talking about what the Devil is doing to them. They are born again, but they are living defeated lives. This is an oxymoron; how can you be born again and live a defeated life? The word "oxymoron" according to Merriam Webster dictionary means: A combination of contradictory or incongruous words (such as cruel kindness); a concept that is made up of contradictory elements.[22]

As the born again, you must stand on the Word of God. You do not have to give up.

> "So, what do you think? With God on our side like this, how can we lose? If God didn't hesitate to put everything on the line for us, embracing our

condition and exposing himself to the worst by sending his own Son, is there anything else he wouldn't gladly and freely do for us? And who would dare even to point a finger? The one who died for us- who was raised to life for us, is in the presence of God at this very moment sticking up for us. Do you think anyone is going to be able to drive a wedge between us and Christ's love for us? There is no way! Not trouble, not hard times, not hatred, not hunger, not homelessness, not bullying threats, not backstabbing, not even the worst sins listed in Scripture.

They kill us in cold blood because they hate you. We're sitting ducks; they pick us off one by one. None of this fazes us because Jesus loves us. I'm absolutely convinced that nothing- nothing living or dead, angelic or demonic, today or tomorrow, high or low, thinkable or unthinkable- absolutely nothing can get between us and God's love because of the way that Jesus our Master has embraced us" (Ephesians 8:31–38 The Message: The Bible in Contemporary Language).

Our Lord and Savior has given us keys of the kingdom to use for our warfare. This is what Jesus says in Matthew 16:19, "And I will give unto thee the keys of the kingdom of heaven, and whatsoever thou shalt bind on earth shall be bound in heaven: and whatsoever thou shalt loose on earth shall be loosed in heaven."

Come on, born again - let's do some binding and loosing!

Binding and loosing is about declaring the terms of entrance into the kingdom of God, and about determining what is or not binding on those who are born again.

What did Jesus mean by the terms "bind" and "loose" as used in Matthew 16:19? The Theological Dictionary of The New Testament states that "deo" and "lou" are the Greek words for binding and loosing. "Deo" means literally or figuratively to bind, "luo" literally or figuratively to loosen.[23] This binding and loosing is neither enchanting nor magical. The customary meaning of the Rabbinic language for "bind' is to forbid, and to "loose" is to permit. I like what the New American Standard Bible translations says in Matthew 16:19 "...whatever you bind on earth shall have been bound in heaven, and whatever you loose on earth shall having been loosed in heaven." The tense of the verbs shows that the disciples were not unilaterally to decide a matter. They did not have the authority of binding heaven to their will or decision. It means that their decision will be in line with what already was God's will on the matter. The disciples were Jesus authoritative spokesmen and that their decisions would be binding. Jesus spoke God's authoritative words and authorized His disciples to speak those words to the body of believers.

For the born again to do some binding and loosing only means that we must come into agreement with God's word on every issue that we are confounded with. God has already set us free from the law of sin and death. Therefore, the Devil has no authority in our life, unless we give it to him.

The Word of God has given us so many tools for warfare. The scripture says; "Thou shalt also decree a thing, and it shall be established unto thee: and the light shall shine upon thy ways" (Job 22:28).

The above verse states that you have to make a decree, and when it is established, light will shine on your way. It means that without issuing that decree, nothing will be established; there will be darkness.

The whole world was in darkness until the Lord God issued a decree. The world was void, dark and He said, "Let there be light." In Hebrew the translation is: "Light, be!" As the born again you too can issue decrees today and something will happen in your life.

What Is a Decree?

According to the dictionary definition, it is an official command, the establishment of a thing in a militant way, or issuing an official order.

- A decree is a decision of a king or government.
- It is an order having the force of the law behind it.

When the born again declares a decree, God is backing it up.

- A decree is an authoritative order or decision to which people have to comply.
- A decree is the determination of someone who has power.

Luke 10:19 says, "Behold, I give unto you power to tread on serpents and scorpions, and over all the power of the enemy: and nothing shall by any means hurt you."

- A decree is to ordain something.
- A decree is to decide what is to be done and what has to take place.

Ecclesiastes 8:4 says, "The King has the last word. Who dares to say to him, 'What are you doing?'" (The Message: The Bible in Contemporary Language).

"And from Jesus Christ, who is the faithful witness, and the first begotten of the dead, and the prince of the kings of the earth. Unto him that loved us, and washed us from our sins in his own blood. And hath made us kings and priests unto God and his Father; to him be glory and dominion forever and ever, Amen" (Revelation 1:5–6).

This above scriptures let us know that God will stand by His word. We do not have to be intimidated by the enemy. God will not let His Word fail.

This means we, the born again, are princes and kings; therefore, we can make decrees. Our kingship is not by selection, nor by election, nor by worldly inheritance, so can't we be voted out of power. Another power can take over a government by a coup and move into power. But the born again are not like that. We are princes and kings by divine appointment. We are not asked to plead with satanic powers to release what they have captured or make a request to them. We are not asked to pacify the enemy; pacifying prayers do not work. We do not have to live defeated lives. Jesus came and took the keys from Satan. We are no longer bound. Revelation 1:18 says, "I am he that liveth, and was dead; and, behold, I am alive for evermore, Amen: And have the keys of hell and of death."

Obedience

To live the life of the born again, you must be obedient to God's Word. We must remember that we are under the authority of the Word of God because we are under the authority of the God who gave it. God and His Word are one.

Obedience to God is hearing and doing the word. James 1:19–25 says:

> "Know this, my beloved brothers: let every person (the born again) be quick to hear, slow to speak, slow to anger;
> for the anger of a man does not produce the righteousness of God.
> Therefore put away all filthiness and rampant wickedness and receive with meekness the implanted word, which is able to save your souls.
> But be doers of the word, and not hearers only, deceiving yourselves.
> For if anyone is a hearer of the word and not a doer, he is like a man who looks intently at his natural face in a mirror.
> For he looks at himself and goes away and at once forgets what he was like.
> But the one who looks into the perfect law, the law of liberty, and perseveres, being no hearer who forgets but a doer who acts, he will be blessed in his doing.
> If anyone thinks he is religious and does not bridle his tongue but deceives his heart, this person's religion is worthless" (ESV).

For the born again, obedience to God's Word begins with active hearing. After getting his hearer's attention with "Know this," James follows with a present imperative (a command calling for continuous action), which says, "Let every person keep on being quick to hear." The born again must keep hearing. There are two other actions James talks about:

- We must avoid talking too much.

- We must avoid reacting harshly in anger.

Both impair one's ability to hear clearly. Further, the born again should:
"Receive with meekness the implanted word" (a command for obedience), in part, by
"Putting away" (past and present) all filthiness and wickedness.

Doing this is similar to having your spiritual ears cleansed, making sure you are actively leaving the vestiges of your old sinful lifestyle that would hinder your hearing of the Word of God.

James is not implying that we can work toward sinless perfection. That would cause us to hear the Word of God in a manner that is completely unhindered by our old way of thinking. He is, however, making clear that we will be better prepared to hear and receive the truth of the word. If we are active both in listening to the word and in removing any known spiritual hindrances.

James lets us know that active hearing is not enough; he gives us another ongoing command, "But be doers of the word." Doers is an active word.

As pastors, we minister the Word of God every week. Many are listening to and hearing the Word. They watch Word TV and listen to the best radio teachers, yet they dishonor God by disobeying the truth they have heard. The end of such a practice, James says, is self-deception.

Ultimately, as the born again, our true submission to God and His Word is not demonstrated by the amount of time we spend listening to God's truth but by the degree to which we live in obedience to it. God has given us His Word as a mirror that shows us an accurate reflection of who we are. Are you reflecting your born again identity? Our response to seeing that reflection, having responded in repentance and faith to Christ, should be gratitude for God's grace and obedient submission to His rule. Jesus said, "If you love me, keep my commandments" (John 14:15).

I remember hearing the following equation:

Stated Belief + Actual Practice = Actual Belief.

If that is true, what does your current obedience to God's Word say about the degree to which you believe it? Does the way you live your life demonstrate consistent, active submission to God and His Word through a lifestyle of ongoing obedience? To live out of your born again self, do you regularly position yourself to hear the Word of God clearly? Do you allow the Word of God to speak to your heart?

CHAPTER THREE

The Comforter

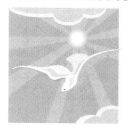

For the purpose of living out of your born again self, Jesus gave you a Helper.

John 14:16 says, "And I will pray the Father, and he shall give you another Comforter, that he may abide with you forever."

Wow! Our Elder Brother prayed to our Father. Jesus knew that the born again could not live out of their born again selves without help. Who is this Comforter and what does it mean "that he may abide"? Let's look at the meaning of the word "abide."

Abide means the following:
Remain, continue, and stay, as in "Abide with me."
Have one's abode; dwell; reside, as in "To abide in my born again self."
Continue in a particular condition, attitude, and relationship.

Abide means that we will never be left alone. Jesus told his disciples and is telling the born again believer today: "I will not leave you comfortless" (John 14:18).

Wow! There is an abiding Presence. Jesus tells us Who and what that abiding presence is when he says in John 14:17, "The Spirit of truth; whom the world cannot receive, because it neither sees Him nor knows Him: but you know Him; for He dwells (abides) with you, and will be in you."

The Spirit of truth is the Holy Spirit. It is the Holy Spirit that brings about rebirth, and regeneration. The world represents all our unregenerate souls. They cannot receive the abiding presence of the Holy Spirit. Jesus gives two reasons why the world cannot receive the Spirit of Truth.

First, it sees Him not:
The world, that is, the world dead in sin and the world dead in their profession (men generally destitute of the life and power of God), must have something that it can see. It cannot receive that which it sees not. Nature, sense, and reason can never go beyond earthly things; thus, while men have no divine faith, they are under the entire influence of their natural minds. As heavenly things can only be seen by heavenly eyes, they cannot receive the things that are invisible. Things must be either presented to their natural eye or be such as their rational understanding can grasp, or they cannot and will not receive it.

The world can receive a religion that consists of forms, rites, and ceremonies, such as I did when I was a practicing Muslim many years ago. My religion of Islam, at that time, was based on performance, as is the religion of millions of people today. A religion that presents itself with a degree of beauty and grandeur to the natural eye will always be readily received by the world. Things that are seen in a religion that consists of forms, rites, and ceremonies are: beautiful buildings, painted windows, pealing organs, melodious choirs, the pomp and parade of an earthly priesthood, and a whole apparatus of religious ceremony; these carry with them something that the natural eye can see and admire.

The world receives all the trappings of external worship because it suits the natural mind and is intelligible to the reasoning faculties. But the quiet, inward, experimental, divine relationship with God, which presents no attractions to the outward eye, but is wrought in the heart by a divine operation, the world cannot receive because it presents nothing that the natural eye can rest upon with pleasure nor does it gratify the general idea of what religion is or should be.

The second reason why the world cannot receive the Spirit of truth is that it does not know him.

The world knows nothing of divine consolation because it knows nothing of spiritual grief and sorrow. Hardened in sin, careless in self-righteousness, or steeped up to the lips in an empty profession, what do men care to know about an inward Comforter? Paul says, "For as the sufferings of Christ abound in us, so our consolation also abounds through Christ" (2 Corinthians 1:5 NKJV). Where there is no suffering, there can be no consolation. Not knowing for themselves anything of the inward consolations of the Spirit, they cannot believe there is such a thing known to the saints (the born again) of God. They do not have the saving knowledge of Jesus Christ. However, we can receive and have the presence of the Holy Spirit, for He lives in our born again self.

John 14:18, "I will not leave you comfortless. I will come to you."

Comfortless

(Strongs #3737) The Greek word is "orphanos," and it means:

- Parentless (this is where we get the word "orphan")
- Bereft of a teacher, guide, or guardian
- To be friendless or desolate

Jesus was saying to his disciples, when I ascend to the Father and you can no longer see me, you must not feel abandoned or orphaned. I will not leave you to face struggles of life alone. I will continue to be your teacher, your friend, and your guide, but I will do it through the ministry of the Holy Spirit. He is sent to the earth to be the Comforter to the born again, which is the body of Christ.

To live out of our born again self, we need a helper, a Comforter.
In John 14; 16–17, Jesus introduced the ministry of the Holy Ghost (Spirit), the Comforter: "And I will pray the father, and he shall give you another Comforter that he may abide with you forever. Even the Spirit of truth…"

The word "comforter" in the Greek (Strongs #3875) is "parakletos," and it literally means someone that has been called to one's side to give aid and assistance.

The Amplified Bible says of John 14:16 "He will give you another Comforter (Counselor, Helper, Intercessor, Advocate, Strengthener, and Standby)…"

The Holy Spirit is all of these things and more. He has been sent to walk by your side and to live within the born again to lead you into a deeper understanding of spiritual truth and infuse you with divine strength to overcome life's struggles. He will also be your partner in prayer, help you communicate your innermost desires to the Lord, and train your heart to hear the voice of God.

To fully comprehend what Jesus was saying, you must understand the meaning of the phrase, "another comforter."

There are two distinct Greek words that are translated as "another" in the New Testament: One word is "heteros" (Strongs #2087), which means another of a different kind and expresses a qualitative difference. For instance, an orange is a fruit and an apple is another kind of fruit. But oranges and apples have different inherent or distinguishing characteristics: they look different and taste different. They are "heteros," or different kinds of fruit.

However, the word translated "another" in John 14:16 is the Greek adjective "allos" (Strongs #243), which means another of the same kind, and denotes a numerical distinction instead of a qualitative difference. In other words, Christ told the disciples that the Holy Spirit will now take his place and provide the same fellowship, the same teaching, and the same guidance that he provided while he was on earth. The same personal relationship that the early disciples had with Jesus can now be ours, through the ministry of the Holy Spirit—He is our Comforter (teacher, guide, guardian, helper, and friend).

The Person of the Holy Spirit

You cannot live out of your born-again self without having a relationship with the Holy Spirit, and you cannot have a relationship without knowing who the Holy Spirit is.

How does the Holy Spirit fit within the Trinity? First John 5:7–8 says, "For there are three that bear witness in heaven: the Father, the Word, and the Holy Spirit; and these three are one. And there are three that bear witness on earth: the Spirit, the water, and the blood; and these three agree as one" (NKJV).

The Holy Spirit is a person, the third member, of the trinity consisting of the Father, the Son, and the Holy Spirit (Holy Ghost).

There are false teachers that teach that the Holy Spirit is God's active force and does not possess a personality; however, the Bible reveals the Holy Spirit to be a "personal" being, possessing every trait of what we call personality, not some "impersonal force" that emanates from God.

The Holy Spirit's Work Manifests Personality:

- **The Holy Spirit Speaks**

- He "expressly says" that some shall depart from the faith. 1 Timothy 4:1 says, "Now the Spirit speaketh expressly, that in the latter times some shall depart from the faith, giving heed to seducing spirits, and doctrines of devils."
- The Spirit spoke and gave directions to Philip in Acts 8:29, "Then the Spirit said unto Philip, 'Go near, and join thyself to his chariot.'"
- He spoke to Peter and about men seeking him in Acts 10:19–20: "While Peter thought on the vision, the Spirit said unto him, Behold, three men seek thee. Arise therefore, and get thee down, and go with them, doubting nothing: for I have sent them."

- **The Holy Spirit Teaches**
  - He was to teach the apostles all things.
  - John 14:26 says, "But the Comforter, which is the Holy Ghost, whom the Father will send in my name, he shall teach you all things, and bring all things to your, remembrance, whatsoever I have said unto you." Please note that Jesus consistently refers to the Holy Spirit as "he," not "it" (implying a personal being, not an impersonal force). John 14:16–17 says, "And I will pray the Father, and he shall give you another Comforter that he may abide with you forever; Even the Spirit of truth; whom the world cannot receive, because it seeth him not, neither knoweth him: but ye know him; for he dwelleth with you, and shall be in you."

The Holy Spirit Possesses Personal Characteristics

- **He has a Mind**
  - The mind of the spirit: "And he that searcheth the hearts knoweth what is the mind of the Spirit..." (Romans 8:27). This suggests thinking on His own.

- **He has Knowledge**
  - He knows the things of God: "For what man knoweth the things of a man, save the spirit of man which is in him? even so the things of God knoweth no man, but the Spirit of God" (1 Corinthians 2:11). Just as the "spirit of man" (a personal being) knows certain things, so does the Holy Spirit have knowledge.

- **He Possesses Affection**
  - Paul speaks of "the love of the Spirit:" "Now I beseech you, brethren, for the Lord Jesus Christ's sake, and for the love of the Spirit..." (Romans 15:30). When have you known of an "impersonal force" that could love?

- **He has a Will**
  - "But all these worketh that one and the same Spirit, dividing to every man severally as He will" (1 Corinthians 12:11). It is the Holy Spirit who decides which person receives which gift.

The Holy Spirit Suffers Personal Slights and Injuries

- **He Can be Grieved**
  - "And grieve not the Holy Spirit of God…" (Ephesians 4:30). He can be made sorrowful through our willful neglect.

- **He Can be Blasphemed**
  - That is, to be spoken evil of, as in attributing His deeds to the works of Satan, the "unforgivable sin:" "Wherefore I say unto you, all manner of sin and blasphemy shall be forgiven unto men: but the blasphemy against the Holy Ghost shall not be forgiven unto men" (Matthew 12:31–32).

- **He Can be Lied To**
  - Ananias and his wife, Sapphira, were guilty of lying to the Holy Spirit: "But Peter said, Ananias, why hath Satan filled thine heart to lie to the Holy Ghost…" (Acts 5:3).

Of Whom Does the Person of the Holy Spirit Speak and to Whom Does He Testify?
  - The Holy Spirit does not speak about Himself. He testifies about Jesus. John 15:26 says "But when the Helper comes, whom I shall send you from the Father; He will testify of Me."

- He shall glorify Jesus.
  - John 16:16–17 says, "A little while, and you will not see me; and again a little while, and you will

see me, because I go to the Father.' Then some of His disciples said among themselves, 'What is this that He says to us, A little while and you will not see me; and again a little while and you will see me; and because I go to the Father?'" (NKJV).

To Know the Holy Spirit, You Must Know His Character

The following are eight additional characteristics of the Holy Spirit:

- He is the Creator
    - "And the Spirit of God moved upon the face of the waters" (Genesis 1:2).

- He is the Convictor
    - "And they, which heard it, being convicted..." (John 8:9).

- He is the Sealer
    - "And grieve not the Holy Spirit of God, whereby ye are sealed unto the day of redemption" (Ephesians 4:30).

- He is the Enabler
    - "And I thank Christ Jesus our Lord, who hath enabled me..." (1 Timothy 1:12).

- He is the Revealer of Divine Truth
    - "But God has revealed them unto us by his Spirit" (1 Corinthians 2:10).

- He is the Builder

- o "And are built upon the foundation of the apostles and prophets, Jesus Christ himself being the chief corner stone; In whom all the building fitly framed together growth unto an holy temple in the Lord" (Ephesians 2:20–22).

- The Holy Spirit Loves
  - o "Now I beseech you, brethren, for the Lord Jesus Christ's sake, and for the love of the Spirit..." (Romans 15:30).

- The Holy Spirit Gives Us Life
  - o It is the spirit that quickenth; the flesh profiteth nothing: the words that I speak unto you, they are spirit, and they are life (John 6:63).

Yielding to the "Comforter"

In John 14:17, Jesus began to teach the disciples how to discern the "Comforter:" "Even the Spirit of truth: whom the world cannot receive, because it seeth Him not, neither knoweth Him: but ye know Him, for He dwelleth with you, and shall be in you."

The world lives by carnal feelings and intellectual reasoning. They only believe what they can see with their physical eyes or prove with their rational minds. Since the Holy Spirit cannot be seen or intellectually discerned, they cannot partake of His ministry. Why? Because they are not born again. The Amplified Bible translates the above verse as, "The world cannot receive (welcome, take to its heart), because it does not see Him or know and recognize Him..."

The words "neither knoweth Him" are translated from the Greek verb "ginosko" (Strongs #1097 New Testament), which means to have firsthand knowledge. Spiros Zodhiates says it means to know experientially or to experience. Vine's Dictionary says that *ginosko* frequently indicates a relation between the person knowing and the object known or to know by observation and experience.[24] In other words, because the world neither sees Him nor has a cognitive relationship with Him, they don't believe the Holy Spirit even exists.

"But ye know him," Jesus said. According to Strongs Greek/Hebrew Concordance, this phrase is translated from the Greek verb #1492 "eido," which is used in the past tense and means to know by perception and to have knowledge of (as in Divine knowledge or revelation). Spiros Zodhiates says that it implies present intuitive knowledge or to know intuitively (which is the ability to perceive or know something without conscious reasoning or physical proof).

The Holy Spirit's ministry cannot be understood by the carnal mind; it must be received through spiritual intuition and spiritual perception. To put it another way, the leadings and prompting of the Spirit can only be understood, initially, by your spirit; you must be born again.

First Corinthians 2:14 tells us that the intellectual man that only relies on empirical (derived from or guided by experience or experiment) knowledge cannot grasp or understand spiritual truth.

"But the natural man..."
Natural man, according to Strongs Greek/Hebrew Concordance, is word #5591 "psuchikos" (the man of the soul or the intellect).

"Receiveth not the things of the Spirit of God: for they are foolishness unto him"
foolishness (Strongs #3472) "moria" (absurd, silly, foolish).

"Rather can he know them, because they are spiritually discerned."
The Amplified translation says that spiritual truth is "nonsense" to the natural and nonspiritual man; he is incapable of understanding because spiritual truth must first be spiritually discerned and appreciated. Jesus said, "You must be born again."

Therefore, God sent the "Comforter," the Holy Spirit, to take up residence in our hearts and impart God's revelation knowledge to our inner man (the born again) to give us spiritual discernment.

CHAPTER FOUR

Prayer, for the Born Again, is a Love Relationship with the Master

We cannot live out of our born-again self apart from prayer. Prayer is the life of the born again. Prayer to the born again is a love relationship with the Master, Jesus Christ. It is worshipping and thanking our Lord for loving us so much that He gave His only begotten Son to die for our sins.

Second Corinthians 5:21 says, "For he hath made him to be sin for us, who knew no sin; that we might be made the righteousness of God in him."

Let me stop here for a moment and explain this verse.

Jesus was made sin; our sins were placed on his body. Jesus was not made *a sinner*, but sin, that is, a sin offering, a sacrifice for sin. The end and design of all this was that we might be made the righteousness of God in Him. In other words, so that we could be placed in right standing with God.

We are justified freely by the grace of God through the redemption, which is in Christ Jesus. Christ knew no sin of his own. However, he was made sin to be sin for us so we, who have no righteousness of our own, are made the righteousness of God in Christ.

The born again understands that when we pray to the Father, we are always thanking Him that He has made Jesus Christ to be sin for us and that we have been made the righteousness of God.

When the born again prays, we are always cognizant that we are in right standing. Because of the blood of the Lamb we can come boldly and approach the throne room of grace. Ephesians 3:12 says, "In whom we have boldness and access with confidence by the faith of him."

I like how the Living Bible translates this verse: "Now we can come fearlessly right into God's presence, assured of his glad welcome when we come with Christ and trust in him."

When the born again prays, he or she knows the following:
- We are justified by faith.
- We have peace.
- We have access to God.
- We have God's grace.
- We rejoice in hope.
- We glories in tribulations.
- We know that tribulation worketh patience.
- We are not ashamed of God's love in our hearts.

"Therefore, being justified by faith, we have peace with God through our Lord Jesus Christ: By whom also we have access by faith into this grace wherein we stand, and rejoice in hope of the glory of God. And not only so, but we glory in tribulations also: knowing that tribulation worketh patience; and patience, experience; and experience, hope: And hope maketh not ashamed; because the love of God is shed abroad in our hearts by the Holy Ghost, which is given unto us" (Romans 5:1–5).

The born again understands that prayer is a time of communing with the Father. We understand that we are in an intense, intimate relationship and there is no greater joy or pleasure than being in His presence.

Psalms 16:11 says, "You will show me the path of life; in your presence is fullness of joy; At your right hand are pleasures forevermore."

The born-again believer also knows that prayer will lead him or her on the path of life. Our joy is full when we are in His presence, because in God hands are pleasures forevermore.

It was an Indescribable Touch. I Knew that It Was Not a Human Touch.

Many years ago, I was moved by the Holy Spirit to dedicate a room in my home as a prayer room, my secret place. I was instructed to build a prayer altar. The altar has three levels, which represent the Father, Son, and the Holy Spirit. I hired a carpenter and had him design the altar as instructed by the Holy Spirit. I then used semitransparent stain to bring color to the altar and saturated the altar in anointing oil. I would play worship music in my secret place 24 hours a day. I spent many hours in that room and on that altar, decreeing and declaring the Word of God.

Through prayer, I have developed an intimate relationship with the Holy Spirit. I have found that he is a person; not a human being, but the third person of the Godhead.

The Holy Spirit is gentle; He will never force Himself on you. The more you spend time with Him, the more He will reveal Himself to you. There is no other joy or peace than being in His presence.

One night while I was asleep, I felt a very gentle touch. It was an indescribable touch. I knew that it was not a human touch. Then I heard a soft, gentle voice, as a whisper, that said, "Come and spend some time with me." I opened my eyes and looked at the clock—it was four o'clock in the morning. I got up, went into my secret place, and kneeled at the altar; the sound of worship music saturated the room, and His presence filled the room. Psalms 17:3 says, "Thou hast proved mine heart; thou hast visited me in the night."

The next night, I again felt this very gentle touch and again heard a soft gentle voice saying, "Come and spend some time with me." I got up and entered into my secret place. It was so wonderful; each night, I would look forward to Him coming into my bedroom and embracing me with that gentle touch. What a time I would spend in His presence! There were also times I would fall asleep on the altar, not wanting to leave His presence. The Psalmist writes: "Do not cast me away from your presence, and do not take your Holy Spirit from me" (Psalm 51:11).

Having the reality of God's presence is not dependent on our being in a particular circumstance or place, but is only dependent on our determination to keep the Lord before us continually.

I remember one day, I received a call while at work. The person that was on the other end of the phone was crying. I asked "What is wrong? Why you are crying?" The person replied, "I entered into your prayer room, and kneeled on your altar, and began to pray, and I could not leave. I began to weep because the room is saturated with His presence." Prior to entering into the room, this person was experiencing depression, and frustration, and just wanted to give up. But praise God, the glory of His presence touched the heart of that person. That person experienced the reality of Psalm 51:12, which say, "Restore to me the joy of your salvation. And uphold me by Your generous Spirit" (NKJV).

As the born again, we must pray without ceasing.
1 Thessalonians 5:17 says, "Rejoice always, pray without ceasing, in everything give thanks; for this is the will of God in Christ Jesus for you" (NKJV).

As the born again, we must have a spirit of dependence that should permeate all we do. This is the very spirit and essence of prayer. Even when we are not speaking consciously to God, there is a deep, abiding dependence on Him that is woven into the heart of the born-again believer. In that sense, we "pray," or have the spirit of prayer, continuously.

One of my greatest joys is to lead an intercessory pray conference call, Monday through Friday from 6:00 a.m. to 6:30a.m. Eastern Standard Time. We have people from difference states call into the line for pray. Please feel free to join the prayer line! **The conference number is 712-432-1500 and the access code is 946337#.**

Conclusion

Living out of your born again self is to know that you are a new creation and have been given a new heart. You have a new beginning. You have a new nature that wants to live for the glory of God. We are made in the image of God, and we are triune beings; we are a spirit, we have a soul, and we live in a body. The born again knows that the new nature is a new spirit. The old sinful nature has been done away with. The born again soul has been set free; we have the ability to choose to live for the glory of God. We choose to have our emotions line up with the will of God, and our bodies belong to God.

As the born again, we must remember: before man fell, it was the spirit, through the soul, that controlled the whole being. When the spirit wanted to do something, it communicated with the soul, and the soul activated the body to follow the order of the spirit.

The soul is potentially the strongest part because both the spirit and the body are incorporated into it; they take it as their personality and are affected by it. But in the beginning, man had not sinned, and the power of the soul was fully under the control of the spirit. The spirit could not drive the body by itself; it had to do so through the soul. We can see this from the book of Luke 1:46–47: "My soul magnifies [present tense] the Lord, And my spirit has rejoiced [perfect tense] in God my savior" (NKJV, emphasis added). This indicates that the spirit must first rejoice before the soul can magnify the Lord. The spirit first communicates rejoicing to the soul, and then the soul expresses this rejoicing throughout the organs of the body. The reason for this is that the soul is the origin of man's personality.

The soul is the master of a person because man's will is part of his soul. When the spirit controls the whole being, it is because the soul has yielded itself and has taken a lower position. Consequence, if the soul rebels, the spirit will not have the power to control it. This is the meaning of "free will" in man. God has given man the right to make his own decisions. He can choose to obey God's will, and he can choose to oppose God's will and, instead, follow the Devil's will. However, it is God's will that the spirit should be the highest part and control the whole being. Yet the main part of man's personality, the will, is of the soul. It has the power to choose to let the spirit rule, to let the body rule, or let the self-rule. Because the soul is so powerful, the Bible calls it "a living soul."

Praise God that we have been given a new life. Paul says, "There is a natural body, and there is a spiritual body...The first man Adam became a living being" (1 Corinthians 15:44–45 NKJV). Adam was created in the image of God, but because of free will, he chose to listen to the Devil. Consequently it caused him to become a natural man, a man of the earth, and a dust man, not a heavenly man. However, Paul continues to say in 1 Corinthians 15:4–9:

> "However, the spiritual is not first, but the natural, and afterward the spiritual. The first man was of the earth, made of dust; the second Man [Jesus] is the Lord from heaven. As was the man of dust, so also

are those who are made of dust [the unregenerate man] and as is the heavenly Man, so also are those who are heavenly [the born again] And as we have borne the image of the man of dust [our old nature], we shall also bear the image of the heavenly man [living out of your born-again self]" (NKJV, emphasis added).

The Need for the Breaking of the Alabaster Flask

We, the born again, are like the ointment of spikenard (pure nard) in the alabaster flask mentioned in Mark 14:5: "A woman came having an alabaster flask of very costly oil of spikenard [pure oil]. Then she broke the flask and poured it on His [Jesus] head." We must realize the need for the breaking of the alabaster flask so that the pure zoë life of God may flow out of the born-again self so that our house will be filled with the odor of the sweet presence of the Holy Spirit.

Your New Heart is Good

Your new heart is good and wants to be with the Lord. You are a saint, made Holy in Christ, and you do have the power to keep sin from overtaking and ruling your life.

As you live in your born again self, God will produce fruit in your life to bless you and glorify him. As you grow out of religion and into a relationship with Christ, you will walk with Him through your life in victory and grace, experiencing Him in all of the ways that you need.

The born again understand that this new nature enables him or her to do sufficient good works by pleasing the father and the Lord Jesus Christ. This is by His grace and power, not merely our own works. Good works with God are the result, or the fruit of salvation.

Ephesians 2:8–10 says, "For by grace are ye saved through faith; and that not of yourselves: it is the gift of God: Not of works, lest any man should boast. For we are his workmanship, created in Christ Jesus unto good works, which God hath before ordained that we should walk in them."

We know that apart from Christ, there is no good thing in us. Anything we do outside of our born again self is not pleasing to God. It is worthless and bears no fruit for God's kingdom.

The most significant part of being born again is that we will live forever. As you live out of your born again self, you will no longer be ruled by your flesh. You understand that you are not just living for today, but you are living for eternity. Everything that you do for Christ will last forever.

The truth you have known and will come to know in your mind can be the same truth in your heart. When that happens, you will experience true freedom in Christ.

Just remember: In your born again self, there is nothing but the love of God reigning in your heart. There is no hate, envy, jealousy, unforgiveness, or pride.

Now all you have to do is make a decision to live your life for Christ.

Remember "I am [that is, the old nature] crucified with Christ: nevertheless I live [the born again] yet not I, [my old self] but Christ lives in me: and the life [zoë, God-kind of life] which I now live in the flesh I live by the faith of the Son of God, who loved me, and gave himself for me" (Galatians 2:20, emphasis added).

112

I am the born again, and I will live for the glory of God. You can too.

Come on, and say the following out loud:

I am born again!

I am a new creation!

I am the born again!

_____

Are you born again? If not, then my question to you is this: If you were to die today, where would you spend eternity?

If God were to ask you, "Why should I let you into my heaven," what would you say?

Can you do enough good deeds to earn eternal life?

You are created as an eternal being. The question is, "Can you answer as to whether you have eternal life or eternal death?"

Now is the time for salvation. Please take a moment to make a decision to accept Jesus Christ as your personal Savior.

Please pray this prayer based on Romans 10: 9–10:

"That if thou shalt confess with thy mouth the Lord Jesus, and shalt believe in thine heart that God hath raised him from the dead, thou shalt be saved. For with the heart man believeth unto righteousness; and with the mouth confession is made unto salvation."

If you prayed this prayer, please e-mail me at alxakj@aol.com.

Another book authored by Alexis Johnson:
I was a Minister in the Nation of Islam. Now I'm a Minister for Christ
Deep Rivers Books, 2009 ISBN #978-1-63269-332-7

This book can be purchased at Amazon.com and is also available for e-book purchase.

Endnotes

Ω

[1] Scripture taken from the New King James Version®. Copyright © 1982 by Thomas Nelson, Inc. All other Scripture quotations are taken from the King James version of the Bible unless otherwise noted.

[2] All references to Greek/Hebrew translations are from the volume by James Strong, Strong's Exhaustive Concordance of the Bible, Hendrickson Publishers, 1988.

[3] Sections 'Rabbi, We Know...' and 'If You Had the Chance...?', are taken from Matthew Henry's Notes section of the PC Study Bible (C) 2008 Biblesoft, Inc. (www.biblesoft.com). Used by permission.

[4] The Holy Bible, English Standard Version® (ESV®), copyright © 2001 by Crossway, a publishing ministry of Good News Publishers. Used by permission. All rights reserved.

[5] From Matthew Henry's Notes section of the PC Study Bible (C) 2008 Biblesoft, Inc. (www.biblesoft.com). Used by permission.

[6] Ibid.

[7] Ibid.

[8] Ibid.

[9] Ibid..

[10] Ibid.

[11] Zodhiates, Spiros Hebrew-Greek Key Word Study Bible, AMG Publishers, 2008.

[12] Holy Bible, New International Version®, NIV®. Copyright © 1973, 1978, 1984, 2011 by Biblical, Inc.™ Used by permission of Zondervan. All rights reserved worldwide.

[13] Amplified® Bible, Copyright © 1954, 1958, 1962, 1964, 1965, 1987 by The Lockman Foundation. Used by permission. (www.Lockman.org)

[14] Romans 8:1-2 Eugene H. Peterson, The Message: The Bible in Contemporary Language. Colorado Springs: NavPress, 2002.

[15] Scripture taken from the NEW AMERICAN STANDARD BIBLE®, Copyright © 1995 by The Lockman Foundation. Used by permission.

[16] Portions of the section 'Know This: The Old Man is Crucified,' taken from Matthew Henry's Notes section of the PC Study Bible (C) 2008 Biblesoft, Inc. (www.biblesoft.com). Used by permission.

[17] New Century Version®. Copyright © 2005 by Thomas Nelson, Inc. Used by permission. All rights reserved.

[18] Leaf, Caroline. Who Switched Off my Brain? Controlling Toxic Thoughts and

Emotions, Thomas Nelson Publishers, 2009, p. 21.

[19] The Holy Bible, New Living Translation, copyright ©2007 by Tyndale House Foundation. Used by permission of Tyndale House Publishers, Inc., Carol Stream, Illinois 60188. All rights reserved.

[20] Dictionary.com. Dictionary.com Unabridged. Random House, Inc. http://dictionary.reference.com/browse/ (accessed: August 24, 2014).

[21] Leaf, Caroline. Who Switched Off my Brain? Controlling Toxic Thoughts and Emotions, Thomas Nelson Publishers, 2009, p. 40.

[22] "Oxymoron." Merriam-Webster.com. 2014. http://www.merriam-webster.com (31 Aug 2014).

[23] Retrieved from Bible Study Tools: http://www.biblestudytools.com

[24] Vine, W. E. Vine's Expository Dictionary of Old and New Testament Words. Nashville, IL: Thomas Nelson Publishers. 1996.

Made in the USA
Lexington, KY
21 September 2019